Breaking Racial Barriers

African Americans in the Harmon Foundation Collection

Preface by DAVID C. DRISKELL
Introduction by TULIZA K. FLEMING

National Portrait Gallery, Smithsonian Institution,
in association with Pomegranate Artbooks, San Francisco

Cover illustration: George Washington Carver by Betsy Graves
Reyneau (1888–1964), oil on canvas, 1942. National Portrait
Gallery, Smithsonian Institution, Washington, D.C.;
transfer from the National Museum of American Art; gift
of the George Washington Carver Memorial Committee

Published by Pomegranate Artbooks
Box 6099, Rohnert Park, California 94927

Pomegranate Europe Ltd.
Fullbridge House, Fullbridge
Maldon, Essex CM9 7LE, England

An exhibition at the National Portrait Gallery,
January 31 to September 14, 1997

Pomegranate Catalog No. A887
ISBN 0-7649-0332-2

Library of Congress Cataloging-in-Publication data are on
file with the Library of Congress.

Designed by Riba Taylor

Printed in Hong Kong

02 01 00 99 98 97 6 5 4 3 2 1

Contents

Mary Beattie Brady: Remembering the Legacy

By David C. Driskell

There are few African American artists of my generation for whom the name Mary Beattie Brady does not bring to remembrance a certain kind of art patronage that we no longer know. And with these remembrances come many colorful stories, some of which recall the peculiarities of an era in American art when black artists had few racially independent sources to turn to in their own communities for the support of their artistry. It is in the context of art patronage that "Miss Brady" as we affectionately called her, the first and only director of the Harmon Foundation from its inception in 1922 until it ceased operations in 1967, came to the aid of African American artists at a very critical time in history. Although Brady did not acknowledge in writing, or verbally to my recollection, the importance of the Harlem Renaissance as a self-made artistic and cultural movement among black writers, visual artists, dancers, and musicians in the 1920s, she nevertheless lent invaluable support to the painters and sculptors whom we now remember as major contributors to the renaissance movement.

Few black artists born after 1930 were the immediate beneficiaries of the Harmon Foundation's select art patronage. In many ways, my own personal experiences as an artist who received limited financial support intermittently from the foundation from 1955 through 1967 are an exception to the rule when one takes into consideration the foundation's history of financial giving, especially that which directly aided artists after the demise of the foundation's Exhibition Program for Negro Artists in the 1920s and the 1930s. Yet a careful review of much of the correspondence that Brady conducted with African American artists teaching at historically black Colleges and universities in the 1950s and thereafter—until the foundation closed in 1967—reveals that

Brady offered little or no financial support to these institutions. She did selectively choose one artist here and there to test her theories on by offering a form of limited help. At times, the help came in the form of a small check. Seldom was more than three hundred dollars given by the foundation for what Brady called "pocket money." It was to be used to conduct "research in social and cultural experimentation" (one of Brady's own phrases). It was through odd circumstances that I became Brady's listening ear and the one individual to whom a measure of support was given from 1955 through 1966.

My time during this eleven-year period was spent teaching art at Talladega College and at Howard University. I received volumes of correspondence from Brady over the first seven years while teaching at Talladega. The remaining four years were spent in the Department of Art at Howard University. It was at Howard that I first met Brady.

I first met Brady in the spring of 1955. It was my senior year at Howard. The occasion of our meeting was Brady's presence at the opening of the William H. Johnson exhibition. I had worked to help install the exhibition as a student assistant to Albert J. Carter, curator of the Howard University Gallery of Art. Although I had read and heard much about Mary Beattie Brady of the Harmon Foundation, the William H. Johnson exhibition offered me the chance to meet her in person. She made an indelible impression on me with her simple style of dress—a black one with a small white collar. She wore no jewelry and no makeup, another trademark of this plain but remarkable woman. She also wore a matching felt hat that seemingly sat flatly on top of her head of lovely white hair.

I was introduced to Brady by James V. Herring, the venerable old scholar who founded the Department of Art at Howard and in whom Brady showed a measure of trust. Thereafter, Miss Brady and I engaged in an exchange of letters that continued over the next twelve years.

Upon my arrival at Talladega College in the fall of 1955, after Claude Clark had resigned his position of associate professor of art there, Miss Brady proceeded to write to me on a weekly basis offering unsolicited advice about how to run the Art Department at Talladega. Much of her advice was helpful, and it laid the groundwork for a more substantial form of help that I was to receive from the Harmon Foundation in later years, particularly after I joined the faculty of the Department of Art at Howard University in September 1962. Immediately upon my arrival at Howard, Brady began to offer advice on a course of action for my teaching art there in the same manner as at Talladega. Much of what Brady offered was sound pedagogical information about principles of art education that she had garnered from reading Vicktor Lowenfield's book *Creative and Mental Growth*. Professor Herring had taught me to be a good listener. And it took many listening hours for one to converse with Miss Brady.

It was after my arrival at Howard University that Brady decided it was time for the foundation to offer me a limited form of financial assistance to further my own career. This assistance came about in the summer of 1964 in the form of a Harmon Foundation Fellowship to do independent study in Europe, a place I had longed to visit. The Harmon Foundation Fellowship amounted to the sum of $1,500. This represented a sizable amount of money, as financial giving goes, from the foundation. But Brady clearly defined the use of the money I received. Six hundred dollars were to be spent on air travel from New York to Athens and from London back to New York. I was issued a first class Eurailpass for three months' travel at a cost of $400. The remaining $500 was given in the form of

a check. It was issued to cover living expenses as I traveled for three months from Greece to England, visiting most of the art historical sites and museums, first in Greece, then Italy, Spain, Holland, France, Denmark, and England, before my return to the United States.

The help Brady offered came about in other unusual ways. Occasionally she offered color reproductions of works by modern European masters such as Cézanne, Matisse, Gauguin, and Van Gogh—prints that she had bought wholesale from Shorewood Press or from the Museum of Modern Art. She wrote long letters of introduction highlighting the importance of color reproductions in places where students did not have easy access to museums. In many ways Brady's formula for art exposure through the study of reproductions in isolated parts of the country, particularly in the South, where many art museums were still segregated or off-limits to African Americans, was the only art exposure some black students received. There were a few times when artists teaching at African American institutions of higher learning were offered commercial mat boards to supplement what Brady called "basic exhibition materials for art appreciation." But it was she who always decided what the basics were. She would ask many questions of her listener, most of which she proceeded to answer before one could respond. Herring was a staunch critic of Brady's administrative policies, but he was pleased to learn that Brady had taken me under her wings and made me one of her star advisees.

Venturing under Brady's wings meant being willing to receive, on a weekly basis, volumes of letters that were almost always six or more pages long in single-spaced type. In these letters, advice about every conceivable thing going on in the art world, from the importance of joining the College Art Association of America, which I did in 1956, to how to cut proper mats for color reproductions, was to be found. According to Professor Herring, I was the only person living at that time who dared endure the "pain and pleasure" of Brady's engaging correspondence and listen, without interrupting, to her long personal conversations. But I benefited in other ways from my association with the Harmon Foundation over the years—ways that added measurably to my appreciation of art, to my own artistic growth, and to my understanding of the world at large.

My close association with Brady was perhaps the last form of patronage in which the foundation expressed real commitment to an individual artist/teacher working at an African American institution of higher learning. But the patronage I received in the form of a Harmon Foundation Fellowship in 1964 had many strings attached to it. Over the years I had proven my loyalty to Brady by turning a listening ear to her unending conversations on the subject of "using art as an instrument for social change" in American society. For Brady, the concept of social change was more about using art as a tool for propaganda than for recognizing the creative impulse of the artist. It was through art that Brady considered herself to be an enlightened crusader for social justice. Being a staunch Republican, she did not like being referred to as a liberal, but she personally perceived herself as being interested in the equality of the races through the plan of integration. She sincerely believed that art could be used as a viable tool in integration.

It was also in this context, of using art as an instrument for social change, that Brady underwrote most of the exhibitions that the Harmon Foundation sponsored for Negro artists from 1926 and the intervening years until 1934, except in 1932 when no exhibition was held. Yet what appears to have been the foundation's most successful exhibition was not the series sponsored in the 1920s and 1930s but one entitled "Portraits of Outstanding Americans of Negro Origin." It opened at the National Museum in Washington in 1944 and generated the kind of response from the public that Brady had hoped for. The exhibi-

tion toured the country during the next ten years with success, and according to Brady, it fostered relevant dialogue "across the unyielding lines of race."

The portraits that were commissioned for the exhibition were executed within the canon of fine portraiture by Laura Wheeler Waring, an African American, and Betsy Graves Reyneau, a European American artist. Both Waring and Reyneau knew Brady's philosophy of art, and they leaned less towards an aesthetic formula when doing the portraits than they did toward creating art with a political reference. Brady did not see her vision for art—that of being used as an instrument for social change—as being anything other than a creative measure of goodwill on her part. The idea that she might be accused of dictating to, or being patronizing to, artists of another race never entered her mind. If such were the case, she would have felt terribly misunderstood. In this sense, Brady may have been somewhat out of touch with reality even though her thought process, one that ideally echoed the saying that "her heart was in the right place," was what most people saw in her dedicated efforts.

Most of the artists of my generation were appreciative of Brady's efforts to confront racism on any level and come to the aid of the cause of integration through all possible ways. But there were those among us who were suspicious of being used by Brady to have their art pursue certain social goals, goals that were not commensurate with a known formula for success in the larger art world. Even I, who never gave up on Brady's ability to help black artists, was somewhat ambivalent about the notion of creating images that addressed the ills of society when other styles in art seemed more marketable. Yet seldom did Brady confront any artist I knew about the relevance of his or her subject matter in her crusade to use art as a tool for social change. But she was unrelenting in her efforts to explain to artists how important it was to their professional careers for them to "keep their ears to the ground," a phrase she often used, meaning that they should listen to the voice of the people rather than follow prevailing styles and fashions in art. In her own influencing voice, Brady managed to dictate taste and style in art while appearing to adhere to a hands-off policy when it came to the subject matter an artist chose to depict.

On numerous occasions, I received voluminous letters from Brady in one week advising me on how artists could improve their public image if they simply "let down their buckets where they are." This saying was one in which Brady paraphrased Tuskegee educator Booker T. Washington, whom she greatly admired as an American icon. She used the portrait exhibition of African Americans, whom she noted had made significant achievements as role models for the Negro race, to validate her belief in racial equality. She had a portfolio of these portraits reproduced for those she called "the common people," believing that any art that found its way into the hearts of ordinary people represented the greatest form of artistry a nation could produce.

Assessing Brady's role in the effort to define the plan of art in African American cultural history is both mysterious and inviting. The mystery of its historical nexus rests principally in the persona of this fascinating Vassar College graduate who chose the socially limiting idea of noblesse oblige over exploiting her own family's wealth—a decision that endeared Brady to the hearts of some, while at the same time causing others to avoid conversation and personal contact with her at all cost.

But the salient role that Brady played in helping many young African American artists realize their creative potential as painters and sculptors is indeed noteworthy in the broad context of art philanthropy. The patronage the Harmon Foundation offered was the most valuable support black artists received prior to the advent of the Works Progress Administration. And while there re-

mained doubts in the minds of some of these artists about Brady's sincerity in fostering the notion that art could be used as an important instrument for social change and to point the way to enlightened dialogue between the races, they nonetheless encouraged loyalty to her and treated her with great respect.

The special support that the Harmon Foundation offered African American artists of my generation and others before me was indeed crucial to our development as artists and teachers in a segregated art world where there were few support services in place to which artists of color could turn. That Mary Beattie Brady was there at the right time to lend a measure of support to African American artists at such a crucial moment in history is an enduring testimony to the legacy of her individual indomitable spirit.

David C. Driskell
Distinguished University Professor of Art
University of Maryland, College Park

Breaking Racial Barriers

By Tuliza K. Fleming

A September 6, 1947, article in the *Minneapolis Star* on the Harmon Foundation's longest-running and most successful art exhibition, "Portraits of Outstanding Americans of Negro Origin," carried the headline "Portraits of Outstanding Negroes Help Break Down Race Prejudice." The exhibition evolved from an experimental program initiated in 1926 by the New York–based Harmon Foundation's founder, real estate developer William E. Harmon, to recognize and promote the overlooked achievements of African Americans, and respond to the increase of racial tension in America. Although the foundation's philanthropic involvement in the promotion—through annual achievement awards and fine art exhibitions of some of the twentieth century's most influential African Americans—is well known within the fields of African American history and art history, precious little information is available about the foundation's portrait exhibition.

The project was initiated under the guidance of the Harmon Foundation's director, Mary Beattie Brady. Brady commissioned Caucasian artist Betsy Graves Reyneau and African American artist Laura Wheeler Waring to create a series of portraits of accomplished contemporary African Americans in the fields of education, art, music, business, science, armed services, law, and government. The exhibition premiered on May 2, 1944, at the Smithsonian Institution, and it then toured around the United States for ten years. Its purpose was to recognize and promote the significant achievements of African Americans, encourage racial tolerance among white Americans, and eradicate the practice of segregation. The Harmon Foundation discontinued the tour following the Supreme Court's 1954 ruling abolishing legal segregation. In *Brown v. Board of Education*, the Court held that the doctrine of "separate but equal"—first set forth in *Plessy v.*

Ferguson in 1896—was unconstitutional and therefore unlawful. The foundation's rationale for closing the exhibition stemmed from its naive assessment that racial tolerance and understanding within the United States had been successfully achieved with this ruling.

The foundation's action is critical in understanding the social purpose of its portrait exhibition. "Portraits of Outstanding Americans of Negro Origin" was not simply an art exhibition. It was a social experiment to reverse racial intolerance, ignorance, and bigotry by illustrating achievements of contemporary African Americans. Although African Americans traditionally used positive visual images to counter racist stereotypes, these were usually distributed only within the black community and therefore did not foster their intended social change. The Harmon Foundation's radical innovation—in its intent to reach a much larger and diverse audience—was its commission of both a black and a white artist to create the portraits for its exhibition. With the Harlem Renaissance of the 1920s, whites began to become interested in the artistic achievements of blacks. These whites were termed "Negrotarians" by contemporary writer Zora Neale Hurston. Historian David Levering Lewis further elaborated on Hurston's terms by dividing Negrotarians into two distinct factions, "earnest humanitarians . . . motivated by an 'amalgam of inherited abolitionism, Christian charity and guilt, social manipulation, political eccentricity, and a certain amount of persiflage'" and those "merely fascinated with the wild abandonment and exotica associated with the 'untamed spirit' of the African American."[1] In the midst of this unique social revolution, in 1922, Caucasian real estate developer William E. Harmon (1862–1928) [Fig. 1] established the Harmon Foundation. Harmon shared many of

Fig. 1. William E. Harmon. Schomburg Center for Research in Black Culture, New York Public Library, New York City

the motivations included in Lewis's humanitarian type of "Negrotarian," and his organization displayed an interest in African American art and culture that directly paralleled the development of the New Negro movement in Harlem. Harmon's interest, however, really emanated from his childhood experiences and was not merely kindled by a decade-long trend. In Oklahoma, his father, who had been a general during the Civil War, accepted a reduction in rank to become a lieutenant in Indian country of the Tenth Colored Cavalry. Harmon spent a great deal of time with the black soldiers under the command of his father. Harmon, who apparently was not especially close to his father, developed a sentimental attachment to the soldiers, who gave him guidance and support. The soldiers taught him how to shoot, and Harmon killed his first buffalo on his twelfth birthday.[2] These experiences had a lasting impact upon his life, instilling his belief that Americans of African descent could weave their way into the total fabric of American society through personal accomplishment.

He established the Harmon Foundation as a small, experimental philanthropic organization to interest his own children in their responsibility for improving America's social conditions. The foundation operated under Harmon's credo that "a gift of service that stimulates self-help can be of as much or more value as a relatively larger gift of money."[3]

Harmon organized his foundation into four main divisions: Playgrounds, Student Loans, Awards for Constructive and Creative Achievement, and Social Research and Experimentation. The goal of the Division of Awards for Constructive and Creative Achievement was to seek out and encourage meritorious but relatively unknown individuals, rather than place additional laurels upon those who had already achieved success and recognition.[4]

The initiation of the Harmon Awards in 1925 was only the first of the foundation's many endeavors to recognize African American achievement. Programs such as the "Exhibition of Works by Negro Artists and Awards" (a by-product of the William E. Harmon Awards), and the much later "Portraits of

Outstanding Americans of Negro Origin," encouraged and publicized African American achievements in business, education, farming, fine arts, literature, music, race relations, religious service, and science.[5]

Although William E. Harmon died in 1928, his foundation continued to function under the careful direction of Mary Beattie Brady [Fig. 2], who—as director of the foundation from 1928 to 1967—preserved his principles of self-help and equality. Brady's devotion to Harmon's vision, coupled with her own unique ideas about racial uplift, proved to be a vital force, enabling the foundation to continue its work with the African American community well into the late 1960s.

Harmon had invited Brady to join the foundation in 1922. Brady was born and raised in Sitka, Alaska. After graduating from Vassar College in about 1910, she returned to Sitka, where she taught with her

Fig. 2. Mary Beattie Brady (seated, left) with Laura Wheeler Waring (seated, right). National Archives, Washington, D.C.

mother at a school for Native American children. She eventually received a degree in journalism from Columbia University, and shortly afterward began her work at the Harmon Foundation.

Mary Brady often recalled the genuine admiration and respect she and Harmon shared for one another. She noted, "He liked me and gradually had confidence in me so he left the foundation for me to run. . . . I liked his approach that he wanted to help people help themselves." Brady quickly learned the internal workings of the foundation, and within four years she became the organization's driving force. After Harmon's death, Mary Beattie Brady would carefully direct the foundation's many diverse programs until its dissolution in 1967.

During World War II and the postwar years, interest in African American integration and assimilation within American society spread at a record pace.

Bolstered by the intensive African American participation in the war effort both at home and overseas; the reversal of federal executive policy of racial segregation, as in the 1941 creation of a Fair Employment Practices Commission; and the continued judicial undermining of the "separate but equal" doctrine, African Americans began earnestly challenging the racial system in the United States.[6] These new social developments, combined with the socially damaging effects of racial stereotypes that had migrated from vaudeville, posters, and trinkets into the extremely popular and powerful arena of Hollywood films, initiated the widespread integrationist and assimilationist movement.

One woman who was especially touched by the United States's incongruous racial policies and proved influential in initiating the portrait exhibition was artist Betsy Graves Reyneau (1888–1964) [Fig. 3]. Born in Battle Creek, Michigan, Reyneau

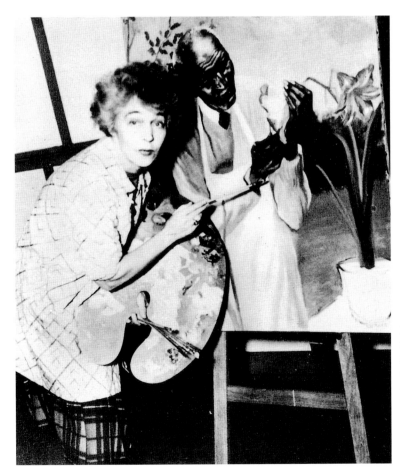

Fig. 3. Betsy Graves Reyneau, circa 1945. From Harmon Foundation photogravure set in the Library of the National Portrait Gallery and National Museum of American Art, Smithsonian Institution, Washington, D.C.

came from a political family. In their activist tradition, Reyneau became involved in various social causes, and by 1931 she had been arrested on three separate occasions for her radical political activity.[7] In addition to being a crusader, Reyneau was also a professional artist. She received the bulk of her artistic training at the Boston Museum School, under the tutelage of painter Frank Duveneck. In 1928 she moved to Europe, where she resided for approximately eleven years. During her years in England, she wrote magazine articles and perfected her quick drawing technique through her work for *The Bookman.*

Reyneau returned to the United States in 1939. She vowed never to paint again, having decided that portrait painting was of little use in a world that was becoming swiftly engulfed by fascism. She soon realized that the United States was just as torn by social inequality and racism as the countries she had fled in Europe.

Reyneau's resolution to abandon painting was short-lived, however. During a visit with an old friend in Florida, she noticed a young African American boy working in the garden. Reyneau became immediately taken with the young man, whom she described as "the most beautiful person I've ever seen, a Negro boy."[8]

Reyneau's penchant for the dramatic, coupled with her genuine concern for social injustice, reflects an interesting blend: a surface fascination that many radical liberals had with African Americans, combined with a genuine concern for their socio-economic welfare. Buoyed by her recently discovered political cause, Reyneau's life was once again filled with purpose. With renewed spirit, she began to wage a new social battle. Her cause was the uplift of African Americans, and her weapon was the creation of a series of portraits of those who set examples for their race.

Reyneau's first portrait of an African American subject was of the young garden worker in Florida, Edward Lee [Fig. 4]. After completing this, Reyneau

claims to have journeyed to Alabama in hopes of capturing the likeness of the famous scientist George Washington Carver. She recalled, *I went to Tuskegee where I met and painted the last portrait of Dr. George Washington Carver. I talked to Dr. Carver about a plan to break down the barrier of ignorance which kept the two races separated. The present exhibition of great Negro citizens who have contributed to our national life is the outcome of that plan.*[9]

In addition to claiming that she had initiated the contact between herself and Carver, Reyneau maintained that she convinced the Smithsonian Institution to accept her portrait of Carver for their National Collection of Fine Arts. She also took credit for inviting African American artist Laura Wheeler Waring to participate in the creation of the Harmon Foundation's exhibition.[10]

In actuality, it is highly unlikely that Reyneau was the motivating force behind any of the events concerning the exhibition, outside of taking the initiative of painting the portrait of Edward Lee. It was the Harmon Foundation that arranged for Reyneau to meet George Washington Carver after she had shown the painting of Lee to Mary Beattie Brady. Reyneau's version of the event, which has been published in numerous articles, appears to have been her own fabrication for publicity purposes.

In a 1953 letter to Margaret Just Butcher, Mary Beattie Brady relayed her version of the origin of the portrait exhibition.[11] She asserted that Reyneau had come into her office one day in the early 1940s, inquiring about assistance with her career. Brady promptly informed her of the Harmon Foundation's policies limiting their endeavors to African American artists. Brady recalled, *I made a number of suggestions to her* [Reyneau] *but I did note the very positive and fine quality of a portrait she had done of a young man down in Florida on the estate of a friend where she had been visiting. His name was Edward Lee. . . .*

A few weeks later I awoke in the middle of the night with a feeling of shame that I had given her such short consideration because it suddenly occurred to me that her work in portraiture might point the way to some very real positive services in wiping out prejudice in this country. I got in touch with her and suggested that she come back for another confab over the luncheon table.

As a result of this, steps were taken to get her down to Tuskegee with the hospitality of the Institute and there she did a life portrait of Dr. George Washington Carver, finished just a few days before he was taken sick and died.[12]

Brady's recollection of these events is more credible, given the Harmon Foundation's long-standing relationship with Tuskegee Institute and in particular with its president, Frederick Douglass Patterson. Reyneau's claim of responsibility for the Smithsonian's acquisition of the Carver portrait is also challenged by Brady: "Through various connections, Mr. Oscar Chapman, then Assistant Secretary of the Interior, became interested and wanted to arrange privately to buy through subscription money that he would raise, the George Washington Carver portrait, with the idea of hanging it permanently in the Smithsonian Institution in the National Museum."[13]

In actuality, Chapman first wanted to illustrate Reyneau's portrait on the cover of a pamphlet in 1943 that was being created to generate attention for a project that Congress granted to the Interior Department. The project's goal was to purchase George Washington Carver's birthplace and make it a national monument. Chapman remembered Reyneau's portrait, and felt that it impressively portrayed Carver's character and life.[14]

Fig. 4. Edward Lee, circa 1942, by Betsy Graves Reyneau. From Harmon Foundation photogravure set in the Library of the National Portrait Gallery and National Museum of American Art, Smithsonian Institution, Washington, D.C.

The circulated pamphlet brought overwhelmingly positive responses to Reyneau's image. The public's reaction to the painting, and to the possibilities of a Carver monument, was so impressive that the department established a committee to purchase the portrait, so that "all the people might have an opportunity to enjoy it, as well as to take an interest in the future development of the George Washington Carver National Monument."[15]

Documents between Chapman, the Smithsonian's Alexander Wetmore (assistant secretary of the Smithsonian Institution), and R. P. Tolman (the National Collection of Fine Arts's acting director) confirm Brady's recollection of the events leading to the Smithsonian's acquisition of the Carver portrait.[16] The National Collection of Fine Arts accepted the donation of the work on the assumption that it would eventually find a place in the permanent collection of the then-proposed National Portrait Gallery.

The Carver portrait—depicting him in one of his famous pastimes, the crossbreeding of amaryllis flowers—was a significant acquisition. It was the last portrait before his death, and it was the first portrait of an African American to be acquired by the Smithsonian Institution.

Brady and Chapman decided that to commemorate such a monumental occurrence, the United States National Museum (then located on Tenth Street and Constitution Avenue in Northwest Washington, D.C.) should house a special exhibition of what was then referred to as "Portraits of Leading American Negro Citizens" in May 1944.[17] Rene d'Harnoncourt, who at that time was general manager of the department's newly created Indian Arts and Crafts Board, arranged for this exhibition under the sponsorship of Secretary of the Interior Harold L. Ickes.[18]

Brady recalled that the decision to mount this exhibition "led to my having the idea of calling Mrs. Laura Wheeler Waring on the telephone at their home in Philadelphia and asking her if she would like to join with Mrs. Reyneau in getting together a collection of portraits by two women."[19] It is unlikely, however, that exhibiting a "collection of portraits by two women" was Brady's most important motivation behind her invitation to Waring. Instead, she was doubtless anticipating the pressure that she and the Harmon Foundation would receive from the black community if they neglected to include an African American artist in a large-scale exhibition celebrating black achievement.

Brady, who apparently felt the need to defend her controversial commission of the white artist Reyneau, explained, *Portraiture* [painted by African Americans] *was so distorted that it was difficult to make any impact on the art-going public. While I feel very hesitant always to try to encourage artists to do something that may not come naturally to them, I do feel that we have a very important responsibility with our criticism to be constructive and to show dignity, leadership and positive values where we can.*[20] Brady's difficulty in finding suitable African American artists probably had less to do with absence of talent than with a lack of interest. Even though the foundation, more than any other philanthropic organization of its time, had access to the most distinguished African American artists of the twentieth century, the proposed portrait project would be time-consuming; the Harmon Foundation did not guarantee payment for the commissions; and the style that Brady desired was both too rigid and too aesthetically unappealing for most artists.

Additionally, the creation of fine art was never Brady's goal for this exhibition. Even though she firmly believed in the persuasive powers of the art object, she also strongly advocated the application of art for propaganda. She once expressed her belief that photographs of an object (even in black and white) were as powerful as painted portraits and could be successfully substituted for them.

Consequently, respected artists such as Aaron Douglas, who worked closely with the foundation and whose oeuvre included portraiture, may have found Brady's offer unappealing, or Brady herself may have found some of the artists to be unsuitable candidates.[21]

Whatever her reasons, Brady, who did realize the necessity of including a black artist in the project, made the politically motivated and precisely calculated decision to pair Caucasian artist Betsy Graves Reyneau with African American artist Laura Wheeler Waring. Brady described this as a symbolic partnership of "two races and two women banded together to fight social injustice."[22] Brady wrote to Frederick Patterson, *I really think Mrs. Reyneau, together with Mrs. Waring, have been rendering a service of growing value in the field of interracial adjustments and I hope that a way may be developed to keep this portrait collection in circulation for a period of years, especially with the idea of using the exhibit as a springboard for activities of various kinds in schools, churches, clubs, labor groups, etc.*[23] Brady's decision was a publicity coup. Throughout the exhibition's ten-year tour,

journalists consistently commented upon its interracial component. Headlines that read "White and Negro Hostesses to Greet Public at Art Show," "Race Harmony, Art Aided in Negro Portrait Exhibit," "Negro Portraits Used to Combat Racism in U.S.," and "Portraits of Outstanding Negroes Help Break Down Race Prejudice" were prevalent during the exhibition's run.

Laura Wheeler Waring (1887–1948) [Fig. 5] was the daughter of the Reverend Robert Wheeler, a Congregational minister, and Mary Freeman Wheeler, a musician and schoolteacher who was one of the first African American women to graduate from Oberlin College.[24] At an early age, Waring displayed a proclivity toward art, which was nurtured by her family and her teachers through high school. Following high school, Waring enrolled in courses at the Pennsylvania Academy of

Fig. 5. Laura Wheeler Waring, circa 1945.
From Harmon Foundation photogravure set in the Library of the National Portrait Gallery and National Museum of American Art, Smithsonian Institution, Washington, D.C.

the Fine Arts in Philadelphia, where she studied under Thomas Anshutz, William Merritt Chase, and Henry McCarter. Six years after entering the academy, Waring was awarded the Cresson Traveling Scholarship, which enabled her to travel throughout most of Western Europe, visiting galleries and finding inspiration.

Upon her return, Waring joined the teaching staff at the Cheyney Training School for Teachers in Pennsylvania to augment her income. Even though she made substantial contributions as an educator, she eventually left Cheyney to return to Europe to study at the Académie de la Grande Chaumière.[25] Waring worked in Paris in 1924 and 1925, interrupting her study periodically to travel through France, the Mediterranean, and Algeria. Shortly after her return to the United States, she was introduced to the work of the Harmon Foundation.[26]

Waring's official involvement with the foundation began in 1926 when she was a replacement juror for the "Exhibition of Works by Negro Artists and Awards." The following year, she participated in the exhibition as a contestant. She subsequently received the Harmon Gold Award and a cash prize of $400 for her contribution to the field of fine arts—the highest Harmon Award ever to have been received by a woman.[27] By this time, Waring had fully established herself as a portraitist, best known for her portraits of African Americans. The five Harmon judges were especially taken with her rendering of Anna Washington Derry, an elderly woman, and *Anita*, a bust of a young woman.[28] Upon receiving the Harmon Award, Waring decided to devote all of her time to her artistic career. Singer and performer Roland E. Hayes observed, "Following the grant to her of the Harmon Gold Award, she has become more enthusiastic about the idea of searching out and the portrayal of Negro types."[29] In her thank-you letter to William Harmon in 1928 she wrote, *Over and above the medal and very generous gift there are results that you have imagined or else you would not have done this. I am writing only to testify that these results are real. . . . May I tell you that I have been planning to make a record of interesting characters of the American Negro in paint. I have*

been invited by a friend in France to bring the exhibit there when it is finished. She will use it largely to create more interest in interracial and international knowledge as she was one who was so much interested in bringing Roland Hayes before the public.[30]

To her close friend W.E.B. Du Bois Waring wrote in 1929 that the exhibition "consists of twelve portraits of American colored women of varied ages and types. Although it was my own exhibition, it had to pass the gallery's sponsors before it was exposed."[31] The Harmon Foundation's knowledge of Waring's exhibition actually points to the possibility that the idea for a portrait exhibition of outstanding African Americans may have originated with her, rather than with Mary Beattie Brady or Betsy Graves Reyneau. According to art historian David C. Driskell—who had formed a close relationship with Brady during the latter part of her life—Brady would often unwittingly adopt the ideas of others and pass them off as her own.[32] Since Waring's letter to Harmon was in the foundation's files, it is entirely possible that Brady read and adopted Waring's ideas from her Paris exhibition.

Waring's African American social connections may have also contributed to Brady's decision to include her in the Harmon exhibition. Her teaching position at Cheyney College—an established venue for African American artists and intellectuals— gave her frequent opportunity to meet the most distinguished African Americans of the period.[33] Such notables as Jessie Fauset, Lillian Evanti, Roland Hayes, Harry T. Burleigh, Claude Mackay, Langston Hughes, James Weldon Johnson, E. Franklin Fraser, Rayford Logan, Meta Warrick Fuller, Henry O. Tanner, Leslie P. Hill, Palmer Hayden, and W.E.B. Du Bois are cited by Waring as friends and social acquaintances in her letters and diaries.

Waring also came into contact with the artistic and intellectual black elite during her stay in Paris. Art historian Theresa Leininger-Miller recorded that Du Bois and Alain Locke *put artists in touch with each other and with other African American contacts in Paris, who made up what Woodruff and others called "the Negro Colony" on the Left Bank in Montparnasse. During the 1920s and 1930s, this group included writers Countee Cullen, Eric Walrond, Langston Hughes, Jessie Fauset, and Claude Mackay; journalist J. A. Rogers; historian Rayford Logan; singers and performers Lillian Evanti, Roland Hayes, Paul Robeson, Florence Embry Jones, Bricktop Ada Smith, and Josephine Baker; and long time resident Tanner. . . . Locke and Du Bois visited the "Negro Colony" in Paris and encouraged others—including Charles Johnson, Walter White, James Weldon Johnson, Harry T. Burleigh, Arthur Schomburg, and John Hope to do the same and to offer their support.* [34]

Waring had a long-lived friendship with W.E.B. Du Bois. They first met in Boston around 1913 during her tenure at the Pennsylvania Academy of the Fine Arts,[35] and their professional relationship had begun in 1918, when she started creating cover and internal illustrations for the journal *Crisis* during Du Bois's term as editor.[36] Her close association with Du Bois, coupled with the fact that she went out of her way to inform him about her Paris portrait exhibition of various types of African American women, suggests that she probably shared his theories about art as an instrument of propaganda.

Waring's political inclinations may have been her primary motivation for participating in the Harmon Foundation's exhibition. A strong civil rights supporter, Waring was a member of both the Urban League and the NAACP. Additionally, her willingness to work with Reyneau, whom she did not particularly like, further suggests her political intent.[37]

Waring accepted Brady's invitation around March 1943 and worked tirelessly throughout the rest of the year. By the following spring, she had completed four new portraits for the exhibition, and to these she added four portraits that she had previously painted.

To my mind Mrs. Betsy Graves Reyneau's portrait exhibit is the first serious artistic effort to illustrate Negro culture and achievement in America through portraits of Negroes who have achieved distinction in their respective fields. Its value in counteracting the Negro stereotypes which the motion picture industry, comic publications and public school text books have imposed upon America cannot be over-estimated. These stereotypes have given America and the world a completely unrealistic and degraded estimate of Negroes which totally unfits the white people affected from dealing with Negroes on an intelligent basis. The exhibit has been a startling success in every city where it has been shown. It reaches all levels, particularly the children in the public schools. It would be a great tragedy if this exhibit has to be taken out of the field due to lack of finances, and I can think of no better way to advance tolerance and understanding and promote good will than by sending this exhibit throughout the country.

—Charles H. Houston
Letter to Evelyn S. Brown
Harmon Foundation, Inc.

The "Special Exhibition of Portraits of Leading American Negro Citizens" opened on May 2, 1944, on a characteristically hot and humid Washington, D.C., summer day. The dedication ceremony for four hundred guests was held at 3:00 p.m. at the National Collection of Fine Arts [Fig. 6]. The exhibition featured eight portraits by Laura Wheeler Waring and fifteen by Betsy Graves Reyneau. Although the dedication of the portrait of George Washington Carver was the primary attraction, twenty-two additional portraits of eminent African Americans graced the walls of the Smithsonian Institution museum. Among those painted by Reyneau, other than of Carver, were William Ayers Campbell (labeled as *Aviator*), Mary McLeod Bethune, Jane Bolin, Charles Drew, William H. Hastie, Charles H. Houston, Eugene

Kinckle Jones, Mordecai W. Johnson, Edward Lee, Alain Leroy Locke, Warren Logan, Paul Robeson, Channing H. Tobias, and Monroe N. Work. Laura Wheeler Waring contributed portraits of Marian Anderson, Harry T. Burleigh, Brigadier General Benjamin Oliver Davis, Lillian Evanti, W.E.B. Du Bois, George Edmund Haynes, James Weldon Johnson, and Dr. Leslie P. Hill.[38]

At the opening ceremony, Oscar Chapman introduced Vice President Henry Wallace, who formally presented the portrait of Carver, on behalf of the George Washington Carver Memorial Committee, to Charles G. Abbott, Secretary of the Smithsonian Institution.[39] The Vice President recalled in his speech that he had first met Carver approximately fifty years ago, and Carver

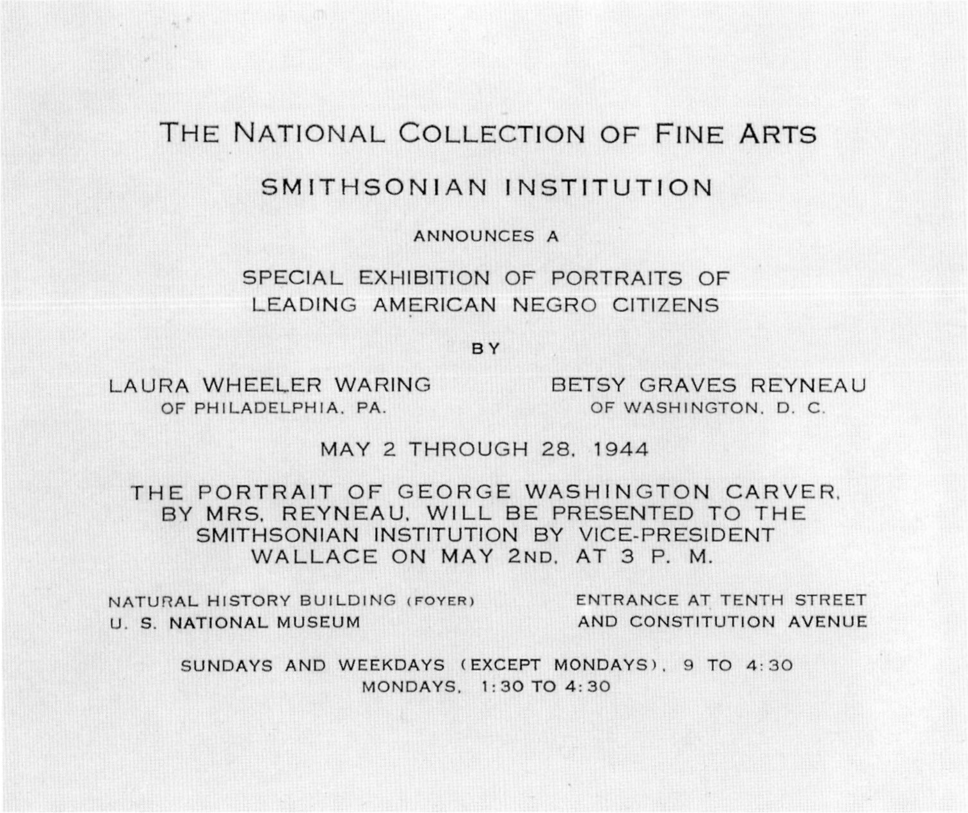

Fig. 6. Announcement card for the Smithsonian's "Special Exhibition of Portraits of Leading American Negro Citizens," May 2–28, 1944. Smithsonian Institution Archives, Washington, D.C.

THE NATIONAL COLLECTION OF FINE ARTS

SMITHSONIAN INSTITUTION

ANNOUNCES A

SPECIAL EXHIBITION OF PORTRAITS OF
LEADING AMERICAN NEGRO CITIZENS

BY

LAURA WHEELER WARING
OF PHILADELPHIA, PA.

BETSY GRAVES REYNEAU
OF WASHINGTON, D. C.

MAY 2 THROUGH 28, 1944

THE PORTRAIT OF GEORGE WASHINGTON CARVER,
BY MRS. REYNEAU, WILL BE PRESENTED TO THE
SMITHSONIAN INSTITUTION BY VICE-PRESIDENT
WALLACE ON MAY 2ND, AT 3 P.M.

NATURAL HISTORY BUILDING (FOYER)
U. S. NATIONAL MUSEUM

ENTRANCE AT TENTH STREET
AND CONSTITUTION AVENUE

SUNDAYS AND WEEKDAYS (EXCEPT MONDAYS), 9 TO 4:30
MONDAYS, 1:30 TO 4:30

was then examining an amaryllis plant. When Wallace became secretary of agriculture, he had asked Carver what he could do to further his research, to which Carver replied that he would appreciate a few amaryllis bulbs. Indicating the portrait, Wallace expressed his hope "that this particular flower...was a descendant of a cross between his own and one contributed by the department."[40]

The opening was attended by several of the exhibition's sitters, including Mordecai Johnson, Charles Houston, Alain Locke, William Hastie, Charles Drew, and General Benjamin Oliver Davis. Eleanor Roosevelt, who earlier that year had seen and liked Reyneau's portraits of Carver and Bethune, also attended the opening.[41] *The first lady, who arrived in the midst of the dedication, made a very dramatic entrance. According to Waring, Mr. Wallace had just begun his talk when there was a cry on the fringe of the crowd, "Make way for the First Lady!" The Vice President stopped in the middle of a word and all eyes were turned toward the entrance. In a few seconds Mrs. Roosevelt eased her way through the throng and took a seat among the participants. Only then did Mr. Wallace resume his speech.*[42] The exhibition opening was by all accounts a success. The following day Eleanor Roosevelt endorsed it in her daily column, writing that the portraits and the achievements of the sitters were of equal interest. By the close of the exhibition, approximately 21,500 spectators had seen it at the United States National Museum.[43] The response was so favorable that the Harmon Foundation decided to tour the exhibition around the country.

Although the objectives of the portrait collection became radically transformed during the exhibition's tour, its basic physical structure remained the same. The layout was simple: Each portrait was accompanied by a brief biography of the sitter. Initially, these biographies were written by well-known and respected Americans, such as Anson Phelps Stokes, Oscar L. Chapman, Arthur B. Spingarn, and William Jay Schieffelin. They were replaced in 1949, however, by a series of more

uniform biographies, compiled and referred to by the Harmon Foundation as "thumb-nail sketches," which were edited and updated by Alain Locke.

The majority of sitters in the collection, in most respects, embodied the goals and aspirations of white Americans. A large percentage of them had attended respected white educational institutions, worked in socially revered occupations, and were admired by both blacks and whites within their fields. The sitters were carefully chosen and screened by the Harmon Foundation before their portraits were commissioned. Although the exact selection process remains unclear, it may have included consultations between Brady and Locke and personal requests from Waring and Reyneau.

Locke was involved with the portrait collection from its initial conception throughout the tour. He served as an unofficial adviser, providing both Brady and Reyneau with direction, contacts, and recommendations for sitters.[44] Between 1943 and 1954, Brady, Locke, and Reyneau regularly corresponded about it. Apparently, both Brady and Reyneau greatly valued Locke's opinion and sought it often. In 1943, for example, before the exhibition opened at the Smithsonian, Brady wrote to Locke, "I think Mrs. Reyneau would be very glad to have you talk over with her the people who should be considered for the portraits for this exhibit. . . . It seems to me that the exhibit is woefully shy on women. Who are the outstanding ones?"[45]

Locke's theories about the worsening status of his race had an impact on the portrait exhibition's presentation. He believed that racism was not an instinctive response of American whites to blacks but was a cultivated phenomenon, designed by the elite to control the less powerful.[46] Locke asserted that African Americans could overcome racism in America though the process of assimilation. He believed that *the ongoing process of cultural exchange and interaction under slavery had made white and black Americans basically similar from a cultural standpoint. Whatever was distinctive about black culture was a product of the particular historical and cultural conditions of black life in America and the cultural characteristics Africans had brought with them on the slave ships.*[47]

Although Locke felt that the concept of race was artificial and that cultural differences were more a product of environment than breeding, he believed that racial identification had certain benefits. Locke recognized that a sense of race, or group, often contributed to group esteem or power, and therefore he did not want to totally eradicate the concept of a black race or culture in the United States.[48]

Following these assumptions, Locke asserted that if African Americans were to improve their social status, they should actively adopt the dominant culture's values while preserving the best attributes of their own. The best way to achieve this goal would be to instill a sense of racial solidarity and loyalty within the "representative classes." According to historian Jeffrey Stewart, *Racial pride for the group, Locke suggested, was the social analogy of self-respect for the individual: it was a powerful ideological tool for building group esteem and solidarity in competitive societies. That race was a biological fiction should not prevent African Americans from appropriating its more legitimate, social meaning—as a social race, as a metaphor for group or national identity—to empower their own development.*[49]

Although Locke's philosophy altered during the Harlem Renaissance in the 1920s, he eventually returned to his original theories in the 1930s, when the ideas of integration and assimilation began to increase in popularity. In 1942, in the introduction to his anthology *When Peoples Meet: A Study in Race and Culture Contacts,* he reiterated his originally held beliefs.[50] Within a year following the book's publication, the Harmon Foundation approached Locke for advice on its exhibition.

The Harmon exhibition was an experiment in the effectiveness of visual association for influencing race relations. Because the exhibition's primary agenda was integration, the personalities represented in it had to represent the values and mores of the dominant race. Personalities who highlighted racial differences or traditionally black professions—such as jazz musicians, rhythmic dancers, or vaudeville comics and performers—were carefully avoided. Therefore, with the exception of Joe Louis (who was the first black boxing champion supported by both races) and the classically trained Marian Anderson and Paul Robeson, the Harmon Foundation commissioned no other portraits of performers.

In addition to highlighting social and professional similarities between blacks and whites, the portraits were purposely painted in an illustrative manner to make them seem familiar to the audience. Brady, who did not want the exhibition to be perceived as an art show, hired both Waring and Reyneau because, in her words, "their technique will not be so startling as to come between viewers and the personality which they are studying in the portrait."[51] Sensitively rendered, the portraits by Waring and Reyneau successfully convey a sense of integrity, honesty, and dignity. Following Locke's assimilationist philosophy, the calm, reassuring, and conservative portraits could simultaneously instill a sense of pride and self-worth in the African American community, attributes that the white community could relate to and admire.

This technique was so successful in establishing interracial empathy that during the exhibition's tour in San Diego in 1948, Reginald Poland, director of the Fine Arts Gallery, where the show was exhibited publicly, commented: *In both* [black and white races] *we find depicted similar qualities in the subjects. In certain of these portraits it is practically impossible to see Negro characteristics in contradistinction to those of whites. . . . what do we especially notice in these portraits? The people portrayed seem quite human, mostly pleasant and friendly, decent men and women—ones who have been trying to achieve, to do something constructive. They seem to have learned the secret of satisfaction in life: being of a real service in the world.*[52]

The Harmon Foundation was well aware of the portraits' effect on the white community. The sitters were specifically chosen, in addition to their personal accomplishments, because they represented Americans whose goals and ambitions were very similar to those of whites. To the white community, these blacks represented decent, hardworking people, who only wanted to be allowed to compete fairly with the majority of white Americans.

Subsequently, if any of the personalities included in the collection contradicted these characteristics through their personal or political actions, the Harmon Foundation would pull them from the exhibition. In 1950 Brady took the portrait of Paul Robeson out of the exhibition because of his association with the Communist Party, basing her decision upon "the fundamental purpose of the exhibit which was to reflect American leadership of the highest type in terms of Americans of Negro

They Are Leaders

SPONSORED BY the Mayor's Interracial Committee, an exhibition of portraits of outstanding Negroes is on view at the Detroit Institute of Arts until Oct. 22. The portraits are shown through arrangement with the Harmon Foundation, established some years ago in New York to increase interest in Negro art. Portraits are to tour the country.

PAUL ROBESON as "Othello," in which he is appearing at the Cass. . . . Now internationally famed as a singer, Robeson was a four-letter man at his alma mater, Rutgers College; picked by Walter Camp as All-American end in 1918.

Photographs from the Harmon Foundation

MARY McLEOD BETHUNE, 40 years ago, founded present Bethune-Cookman College at Daytona, Fla., one of Deep South's major schools. In 1934 Roosevelt named her head of Negro NYA. Mrs. Bethune organized, heads National Council of Negro Women.

AMHERST AND Harvard Law School alumnus, Judge William H. Hastie is dean of Howard University's Law School, former aide to Secretary of War, district court judge in the Virgin Islands and assistant solicitor of Department of Interior.

Fig. 7. Announcement of the Harmon Foundation exhibition in a Detroit newspaper, 1944. From Harmon Foundation publicity scrapbook in the Library of the National Portrait Gallery and National Museum of American Art, Smithsonian Institution, Washington, D.C.

ancestry."[53] The promotion of these personalities as Americans first and African Americans second was precisely Brady's agenda.

The original portrait exhibition at the Smithsonian was a fairly passive vehicle of social reform. However, after the dedication of the George Washington Carver portrait, it quickly evolved into an agent of social activism and protest. This evolution was engineered by Mary Beattie Brady. She believed not only that the achievements, integrity, and dignity of distinguished African Americans could be successfully communicated through portraiture, but also that the Harmon Foundation portrait collection should serve as a cultural springboard from which a series of activities, concentrating on the exchange of knowledge and ideas between white and black communities, would develop: *I have always felt that unless they [the hosting community] were doing something themselves with the material using it as a point of departure that the results were less than optimal. I feel for instance that in the colleges, and in high schools and even grade schools, it would be desirable to work out plans so that there could be a special shelf of books on and by Americans of Negro descent, the African scene, racial adjustment everywhere. I believe that there should be bulletin boards stressing all during the year achievements, and what leads to achievements, and that while in respect to the adjustment of our great minority groups, that this should be an even broader approach.*[54] Brady's revolutionary vision of multicultural community exchange and education was far ahead of her time. During the 1940s and 1950s, the concept of promoting African American accomplishment within public educational facilities, museums, or even black majority schools, outside of the set-aside "Negro History Week" in February, was virtually nonexistent.

Fig. 8. Betsy Graves Reyneau and several schoolchildren viewing Reyneau's portrait of Jane Bolin.

Because the collection specifically aspired to transform white racist attitudes, "Portraits of Outstanding Americans of Negro Origin" purposely avoided traditional African American venues during its tour. Interestingly, the collection bypassed white southern venues as well [see Exhibition Venues list on page 116]. Although the Harmon Foundation does not definitively document the rationale behind its choice of venues, from the existing correspondence concerning the exhibition, several assumptions can be formulated.

In a letter responding to Tuskegee Institute president Frederick Douglass Patterson's request to house the exhibition, Brady explained her belief that the exhibition would do a far better job in alleviating racial tension in venues with a greater interracial constituency than would be found at a majority African American institution.[55] Brady would also have been reticent to grant white southern institutions, which were legally required to institute segregationist practices, the right to house the show. However, the Harmon Foundation records do not indicate that any southern venue outside of Tuskegee, black or white, ever attempted to sponsor the exhibition.

For the venues that the Harmon Foundation did accept as appropriate, every effort was taken to increase racial understanding and communication within that community. In addition to displaying the portraits, the Harmon Foundation implemented new and radical techniques to promote a sense of cultural awareness and interracial cooperation. The two women responsible for executing these techniques were Betsy Graves Reyneau and African American social activist Bella Taylor McKnight.

Laura Wheeler Waring did not actively participate in the traveling exhibition. Unlike Reyneau—who divorced early in life and was unencumbered by her domestic or professional life—Waring was married and extremely devoted to her husband. She held the position of head of the Art Department at Cheyney State College, which left her no

opportunity for the extensive travel that proper promotion of the tour required. Furthermore, although Waring was a witty and insightful conversationalist and extremely dedicated to her own work and to civil rights, she tended to shy away from public speaking and self-promotion.[56] Waring also became terminally ill a few years into the exhibition's tour, and even though she fought valiantly and continued to paint every day she was able, she died in 1948.

Given these circumstances, Reyneau traveled with the exhibition as the sole representative artist. She immediately made her presence felt through her characteristically dramatic and aggressive personality. Reyneau spoke out forcefully against racial injustice on the exhibition's very first stop, in Detroit. When the *Michigan Chronicle* covered the exhibition in 1944, it ran the headline "Whites Called 'Problem Race' by Portrait Painter." The article quotes Reyneau: "The race problem now confronting us is that of the white or pink race. The fight is between the progressive liberals and the status Quo-ers."[57]

Reyneau's ability to directly challenge white Americans to reassess their beliefs about African Americans was a product both of her feisty personality and her privileged status as an educated, socially connected, independent white woman in America. Throughout the traveling exhibition, Reyneau spoke out against fascism in America, challenged both the South and the North to rectify the problem of discrimination, criticized American artists for failing to recognize some of the country's great men and women because of their race, and disparaged the general lack of knowledge surrounding the history and contemporary life of African Americans.

Reyneau's speeches were often embellished with her personal recollections. She recalled one incident *in a Southern drugstore where a white policeman was discourteous to a Negro woman. She followed him to the street and called him "just another Nazi" to his face. To her audience she [Reyneau] emphasized, "Never, never let the no's have it!*

There is little difference between the south and the north and fascist Italy and Germany on racial issues."[58] Constructed to arouse controversy, Reyneau's speeches did not spare political sensitivities. Described by journalists as a "friendly militant," "fiery," and even a "ball of fire," the small, slender artist created a sensation.

Reyneau's blunt tactics, however, did not always appeal to the communities to which the exhibition traveled. On many occasions when a more diplomatic and less emotionally charged approach would be more effective, Bella Taylor McKnight took over.

The Harmon Foundation appointed McKnight as the portrait collection's curator as soon as the decision was made to tour the exhibition. A former member of the Young Women's Christian Association, the United States Civil Service Commission, and the staff of the National Y.W.C.A., McKnight filled a vital role during the exhibition's tour.[59] Although her official title was portrait curator, in reality her role was far more extensive. McKnight was responsible for booking the exhibition's venues, serving as hostess during opening ceremonies, giving tours, conducting interviews, and advertising and promoting the show. In addition, she also served as the foundation's liaison to the nation's varied communities, both white and black.

As the only black woman involved in the exhibition, McKnight, in the public's eye, symbolically took Waring's place. During opening ceremonies and special events related to the exhibition, both McKnight and Reyneau worked together to greet guests, attend related social functions, conduct tours, and give lectures. This symbolic partnership between black and white conveyed the exhibition's message eloquently. In many of the cities where the exhibition traveled, interest focused on the novelty of McKnight and Reyneau's equal status as hostesses for the opening ceremonies.

McKnight also added an essential balance to Reyneau's left-wing bias. McKnight was adept at maneuvering through the racial politics that often

befell the exhibition project. Although her political savvy was undoubtedly enhanced during her years of involvement in the arena of social activism, it may also have developed as a basic survival technique for a black woman in a racially segregated society.

McKnight's less aggressive and abrasive personality gave her an edge over the fiery Reyneau in interpersonal and community relations. She was proficient in convincing reticent museums and institutions to host the controversial exhibition, and Reyneau conceded that of the two of them, McKnight "has been more effective in breaking down the resistance of certain art museums."[60] These differences in the two women's public personae may explain why McKnight was far more involved with the organization of community activities related to the portrait exhibition.

As Brady envisioned, "Portraits of Outstanding Americans of Negro Origin" did eventually become a starting point for related educational and interracial activities. As early as December 1945, the Harmon Foundation developed a series of photogravures featuring twenty-two of the portraits in the exhibition. The photogravures were distributed to the public individually or in portfolio sets for display at schools, libraries, churches, clubs, and private homes.[61]

The photogravure set proved to be fairly popular. Although the actual exhibition was the focal point of community activity, whenever possible McKnight would place the reproductions in public libraries, where they would be prominently displayed along with related publications by or about their subjects.

Reaction to McKnight's community-based interactive project was overwhelmingly positive. A December 1946 review in *The Crisis* includes a reference to the library display while the show was in Cleveland. The article reveals that the display was almost as effective and popular as the actual exhibition: *people seeing the books often viewed them with the feeling that here was a display that could be used in their own organizations, be they schools, churches, or settlement houses. It was the kind of thing which might be immediately, and indeed, continuously available to them, while the portraits, in all their glory of color and vitality, would be there only for a while.*[62] Indeed, numerous individuals and organizations ordered the photogravures for many of the same reasons stated in *The Crisis* review.[63]

The combination of community involvement and the tireless efforts of Brady, Reyneau, and McKnight made "Portraits of Outstanding Americans of Negro Origin" an unprecedented hit in almost every city where it traveled. The NAACP, the Urban League, local interracial committees, and other integrationist organizations immediately recognized the exhibition's educational benefits and wholeheartedly supported its goals by organizing interracial teas, which generally included a lecture given by McKnight or Reyneau; sponsoring opening ceremonies; hosting discussion panels on the integration of the African American into mainstream American life; and purchasing related materials distributed by the foundation.[64]

In addition to the photogravure set, the Harmon Foundation had produced an educational filmstrip. The filmstrip—accompanied by "thumb-nail sketches" describing the accomplishments of each of the sitters—contained thirty-six selected portraits from the collection and was generally distributed to schools and other educational organizations. The foundation also provided photographic reproductions of any of the portraits not included in the photogravure set, as well as enlargements for individuals or organizations.

After ten long years of fighting for the integration of African Americans in all facets of life within the United States, the Supreme Court decided in 1954 to legally abolish segregation in all of its manifestations throughout the country. In the eyes of Mary Beattie Brady, the Harmon Foundation's mission was hereby accomplished, and its job was over. She officially closed the exhibition, declaring that it was "high time that organizations where the

impetus and leadership is largely American of Negro origin carry the ball of constructive activities along these lines."[65] Although the Supreme Court decision may have officially sealed the portrait exhibition's fate, the steady decrease in public interest had effectively stopped the tour almost two years earlier.

Regardless of the underlying reasons for its discontinuation, "Portraits of Outstanding Americans of Negro Origin" was an innovative and far-reaching experiment in social reform. During the ten years the exhibition was active, the Harmon Foundation was instrumental in the Smithsonian Institution's acquisition of the portrait of George Washington Carver; organized a revolutionary exhibition of portraits created for the express purpose of desegregating America; garnered impressive support by both black and white organizations and individuals around the nation; exposed America to the underrepresented accomplishments of African Americans in the professional fields of education, science, law, government, and religion; and, within each traveling venue, established a strong base of interracial community involvement through interactive programs, projects, and events.

Structurally and visually, "Portraits of Outstanding Americans of Negro Origin" also established a precedent. Even though African Americans had long created their own portraiture to counteract stereotypes by whites, this portraiture was only seen by the black community because of the limitations of distribution. The Harmon Foundation's portrait collection, however, received unprecedented national exposure, reaching both black and white audiences. Interestingly, although both blacks and whites supported the exhibition and its social agenda, the reasons behind their support were markedly different.

For the African American elite, the exhibition represented an opportunity for blacks to be presented on a national forum in a positive and dignified manner that represented the diversity within the culture. It illustrated a commonality of values between blacks and whites, yet promoted a strong allegiance to African American racial identity. For instance, the sitters appeared in an assortment of shades and colors, lived in different parts of the country, and came from various economic and social backgrounds. They were all formally educated, many in the highest-ranking colleges and universities in the country, and all achieved unusual prominence within their respective fields. However, notwithstanding their success and achievement in a white-dominated culture, all of the sitters utilized their talents for the betterment of the African American community.

For whites, the presentation of these distinguished African Americans reassured those who were ambivalent about the potential effects of desegregation. Popular media and literature had indoctrinated many whites into the belief that African Americans represented the antithesis of everything they valued. Blacks were believed to be less capable, unintelligent, violent, sex-starved, immoral, and unpredictable. "Portraits of Outstanding Americans of Negro Origin" counteracted these myths through the calm, friendly, and dignified portrayal of their subjects. Moreover, the accompanying biographies and interracial activities further erased ingrained stereotypes by giving whites a glimpse of the personal and professional lives of the sitters and by exposing whites, on an equal basis and in a non-threatening social situation, to the blacks within their own community.

Although it is evident today that the Harmon Foundation's exhibition did not eradicate racial fears and tension within America, it did successfully expose and improve the perception and recognition of African American achievement and contribution to this nation.

Notes

1. "Negrotarians" was writer Zora Neale Hurston's term for "whites who specialized in African-American uplift." For further discussion, see David Levering Lewis, *When Harlem Was in Vogue* (New York: Oxford University Press, 1989), pp. 98–101.

2. Harmon Foundation, Inc., "Informal Notes on the Funding Activities of the Harmon Foundation, Inc.," archives of David C. Driskell; Mary Beattie Brady, interview by Jay Buell and Grant Spradling, Tricentennial Organization, October 19, 1981, archives of David C. Driskell.

3. Harmon Foundation, "The Harmon Foundation: A Brief statement of its origin and activities," January 22, 1953, Harmon Foundation Collection, National Portrait Gallery, Smithsonian Institution, Washington, D.C.

4. The principles surrounding the third division proved influential in the developing of venues for the acknowledgment for African Americans of achievement. For additional information, see Harmon Foundation, "Activities of the Harmon Foundation Incorporated," 1929, Harmon Foundation Collection, National Portrait Gallery.

5. The "Exhibition of Works by Negro Artists and Awards" was established in 1927 for the purpose of "acquainting and interesting the public more generally in the creative accomplishments in fine arts by Negroes. It is thus hoped not only to encourage the Negro in creative expression of a high order, but to assist him to a more sound and satisfactory economic position in the field of art." Harmon Foundation, *Catalogue of an Exhibition of Paintings and Sculpture by American Negro Artists at the National Gallery of Art*, May 16–29, 1929, p. 3, collection of Dorothy Porter Wesley. For further information regarding this exhibition, see Gary A. Reynolds and Beryl J. Wright, *Against the Odds: African American Artists and the Harmon Foundation* (New Jersey: The Newark Museum, 1989).

6. Abby Arthur Johnson and Ronald Mayberry Johnson, *Propaganda and Aesthetics: The Literary Politics of Afro-American Magazines in the Twentieth Century* (Amherst: The University of Massachusetts Press, 1979), p. 125.

7. As a result of her spirited picketing for the National Woman's Party in 1917, she was among the dozen or so women arrested and placed in a workhouse. In the 1920s she was arrested during a Margaret Sanger demonstration, and then again in 1931 for stopping two Detroit policemen from beating an African American. "This Is Cleveland: The Editor's Column," *Cleveland News,* March 6, 1946, Harmon Foundation Collection, National Portrait Gallery.

8. *Michigan Chronicle*, "Whites Called 'Problem Race' by Portrait Painter," October 21, 1944, Harmon Foundation Collection, National Portrait Gallery.

9. "Minneapolis Art Institute to Show Portraits of Famous Negro Leaders," *St. Paul Recorder,* August 29, 1947, Harmon Foundation Collection, National Portrait Gallery.

10. "Negro Portraits Used to Combat Racism in U.S.," *New York Herald Tribune*, April 13, 1947, Harmon Foundation Collection, National Portrait Gallery.

11. Brady to Butcher, March 30, 1953, archives of David C. Driskell.

12. Reyneau painted the portrait of Carver in the autumn of 1942; Carver died on January 5, 1943. Brady to Butcher, March 30, 1953, archives of David C. Driskell.

13. Brady to Butcher, March 30, 1953, archives of David C. Driskell.

14. Oscar L. Chapman to R. P. Tolman, May 12, 1944, Record Unit 311, Smithsonian Institution Archives.

15. The George Washington Carver Memorial Committee included Mrs. Lauchlin Currie (Chairman), Mrs. Oscar Chapman, and Mr. Melvin Hildreth. Among those who contributed the required $1,000 to purchase the portrait were: Mrs. Caroline Parker, Colonel Julius Peyser, Mr. Edwin Pauley, Mr. Malcolm Ross, Mrs. Charles Brannan, Mr. Tom Corcoran, Mrs. Lauchlin Currie, Mrs. Oscar Chapman, and Mr. Melvin Hildreth. *Ibid.*

16. The bulk of the correspondence relating to the Smithsonian's acquisition of the Carver portrait is located in the Smithsonian Institution Archives, Record Unit 311, and the National Portrait Gallery Registrar's file on George Washington Carver.

17. Once the exhibition began touring the United States, the name changed to "Portraits of Outstanding Americans of Negro Origin." Alexander Wetmore to Oscar L. Chapman, November 15, 1943, Record Unit 311, Smithsonian Institution Archives.

18. John C. Garraty and Mark C. Carnes, eds., *Dictionary of American Biography: Supplement Eight, 1966–1970* (New York: Charles Scribner's Sons, 1988), p. 126. Betsy Graves Reyneau to Alexander Wetmore, March 23, 1944, Record Unit 311, Smithsonian Institution Archives.

19. Brady to Butcher, March 30, 1953, archives of David C. Driskell.

20. *Ibid.*

21. Brady may not have chosen Douglas for the exhibition for personal reasons. She once stated in an interview that she felt that Douglas did not work up to his fullest potential. Mary Beattie Brady, interview by Jay Buell and Grant Spradling, Tricentennial Organization, October 19, 1981, archives of David C. Driskell.

22. Brady to Margaret Butcher, March 30, 1953, archives of David C. Driskell.

23. Brady to Frederick Douglass Patterson, December 21, 1945, archives of David C. Driskell.

24. Harmon Foundation, "Laura Wheeler Waring (deceased)," January 1950, Harmon Foundation Collection, National Portrait Gallery.

25. Waring established a basic art course for the State Teacher's College of Pennsylvania. Howard University Gallery of Art, *In Memoriam: Laura Wheeler Waring, 1887–1948*, May and June 1949, collection of Dorothy Porter Wesley.

26. *Ibid.*

27. Brady to Waring, February 7, 1928, Harmon Foundation Collection, Manuscript Division, Library of Congress, Washington, D.C.

28. John Simon Guggenheim Memorial Foundation, "Confidential Report of Candidate for Fellowship," November 12, 1928, Harmon Foundation Collection, Manuscript Division, Library of Congress.

29. *Ibid.*

30. Waring to William Harmon, February 26, 1928, Harmon Foundation Collection, Manuscript Division, Library of Congress.

31. Du Bois, Harmon, Leslie Pinckney Hill (Waring's boss at Cheyney College), and Waring's husband were the only people Waring told about her exhibition.

32. David C. Driskell, interview by Tuliza Fleming, July 15, 1995.

33. Because of segregation, venues for African American artists wishing to perform for black audiences were few. Institutions of higher learning that had appropriate facilities, such as Cheyney College, were often included as part of the black travel circuit.

34. Theresa Leininger-Miller, "'The Negro Colony' in Paris: 1922–1934," *Paris Connections: African American Artists in Paris* (San Francisco: Bomani Gallery and Q.E.D. Press, 1922), p. 18.

35. Madeline Wheeler Murphy, conversation with author, August 26, 1996.

36. David Levering Lewis, conversation with author, August 20, 1996.

37. Walter Waring, interview by Madeline Wheeler Murphy, collection of Madeline Wheeler Murphy.

38. Although the Harmon Foundation had arranged for all of Reyneau's portraits with the exception of her portrait of Edward Lee, four of Waring's portraits had been painted prior to her involvement with the portrait exhibition (Burleigh, Davis, Johnson, and Hill). Except for Anderson, Waring knew all of the sitters she painted for the portrait exhibition personally. Laura Wheeler Waring, "Paintings of Negro Americans," *Pulse*, circa May 6, 1944. Laura Wheeler Waring, diary entry, May 2, 1944, collection of Madeline Wheeler Murphy; exhibition invitation and portrait listing, Record Unit 311, Smithsonian Institution Archives.

39. Laura Wheeler Waring, "Paintings of Negro Americans," *Pulse*, circa May 6, 1944, p. 3.

40. "Wallace Pays Tribute To Dr. Carver as He Presents Portrait," *Washington Star*, May 3, 1944.

41. In her column, "My Day," Roosevelt mentions how she "stopped in at the office of the Assistant Secretary of the Interior to see a portrait of Dr. Carver by Miss Betsy Reyneau. It was done only a month before Dr. Carver's death and it is a delightful portrait. She has also painted one of Mrs. Mary McLeod Bethune, which is extremely good." Eleanor Roosevelt, "My Day: Navy Combat Artists Vividly Picture Action in Pacific," *Washington Daily News*, February 3, 1944.

42. Laura Wheeler Waring, "Paintings of Negro Americans," *Pulse*, circa May 6, 1944, p. 34.

43. Eleanor Roosevelt, "My Day: 16-Year-Old-Girl Pens Winning Verse on Dr. G. W. Carver," *Washington Daily News*, May 4, 1944; R. P. Tolman to Betsy Graves Reyneau, July 27, 1944, Record Unit 311, Smithsonian Institution Archives.

44. I use the word unofficial here because Locke is never publicly given credit for his role in the formation of the portrait exhibition. This may have been by his design, for during this time period, he often supported projects with which he did not necessarily want to be associated.

45. Brady to Alain Locke, October 1, 1943, Alain Locke Papers, 164–15, file 36, Moorland-Spingarn Research Center, Howard University.

46. For further discussion regarding Locke's lecture series on race relations in the United States, see Alain Leroy Locke, *Race Contacts and Interracial Relations*, ed. Jeffrey C. Stewart (Washington, D.C.: Howard University Press, 1992), p. xxi.

47. *Ibid.*, p. xxv.

48. *Ibid.*

49. *Ibid.*, p. xxxii.

50. *Ibid.*, pp. xlvii–xlviii.

51. Brady to Locke, October 1, 1943, Alain Locke Papers, 164–15, file 36, Moorland-Spingarn Research Center, Howard University.

52. "Portraits Reveal Stature of Race, Director Notes," *San Diego Union*, May 30, 1948, Harmon Foundation Scrapbook, National Portrait Gallery.

53. Brady to Dr. John A. Kenny, June 29, 1951, Harmon Foundation Scrapbook, National Portrait Gallery.

54. Brady to Laplois Ashford (youth secretary to the Youth Council and College Division, National Association for the Advancement of Colored People), April 2, 1963, archives of David C. Driskell.

55. Originally, Tuskegee Institute requested the exhibition in 1946. Because of Brady's integrationist ambition, she deferred sending the exhibition to Alabama until 1950. Brady to Frederick Douglass Patterson, February 25, 1946, archives of David C. Driskell.

56. Walter Waring, interview by Madeline Wheeler Murphy, May 25, 1973, collection of Madeline Wheeler Murphy.

57. "Whites Called 'Problem Race' By Portrait Painter," *Michigan Chronicle*, October 21, 1944, Harmon Foundation Scrapbook, National Portrait Gallery.

58. *Ibid.*

59. "Mrs. McKnight, In Speech at RO, Says Democracy Not under Test," *Palo Alto Times*, February 11, 1949, Harmon Foundation Scrapbook, National Portrait Gallery.

60. "Noteworthy Americans Included in Collection of Thirty Paintings," 1947, Harmon Foundation Scrapbook, National Portrait Gallery.

61. Brady to Frederick Douglass Patterson, December 21, 1945, archives of David C. Driskell.

62. Fern Long, "A Cultural Operation Crossroads," reprint from *The Crisis*, December 1946, p. 368.

63. According to Brady, within the first few months of production, the National Tuberculosis Association ordered 600 copies for mailing and the Friendship Press of the Missionary Education Movement ordered a special printing of ten portraits, 5,000 of each, for their study program for February 1946. Brady to Frederick Douglass Patterson, December 21, 1945, archives of David C. Driskell.

64. Harmon Foundation Scrapbook, National Portrait Gallery.

65. Brady to Carl Mydans (Mamaroneck National Association for the Advancement of Colored People Branch), January 28, 1964, archives of David C. Driskell.

Catalogue

When the Harmon Foundation discontinued the tour following the 1954 Supreme Court decision, the majority of the collection of "Portraits of Outstanding Americans of Negro Origin" was placed in indefinite storage. Although the Harmon Foundation, and Betsy Graves Reyneau (1888–1964) in particular, actively sought to place the collection within a permanent exhibition space, they did not find a suitable repository until 1966.

In June of 1966, arrangements to transfer ownership of the portraits commenced between the Harmon Foundation and the newly established Smithsonian museum, the National Portrait Gallery. After a series of correspondence and meetings between the Harmon Foundation's assistant secretary, Evelyn S. Brown, its director, Mary Beattie Brady, and Charles Nagel, the director of the National Portrait Gallery, forty-one of the original fifty portraits exhibited were acquired by the Gallery in 1967. The majority of portraits that did not enter the National Portrait Gallery's collection were painted by Laura Wheeler Waring (1887–1948) and were not owned by the Harmon Foundation. Her portraits include those of Raymond Alexander (1897–?), lawyer; Sadie Alexander (1898–?), lawyer; Brigadier General Benjamin Oliver Davis (1887–1970); Lillian Evanti (1891–1967), coloratura and lyric soprano; George Edmund Haynes (1875–1960), co-founder and executive secretary of the Department of Race Relations of the Federal Council of Churches; and Leslie Pinckney Hill (1880–1960), educator and author. Among those painted by Reyneau that were not included in the National Portrait Gallery's 1967 acquisition are: her first portrait of Charles Drew (1904–1950), medical doctor and scientist; Eugene Kinckle Jones (1884–1951), executive director of the Urban League, 1918–1941; Private Edward Lee; and Mary Church

Terrell (1863–1954). These portraits were not donated to the Smithsonian because they had either been purchased by individuals or organizations in the years prior to 1966, or, as in the case of the portraits of Eugene Kinckle Jones and Mary Church Terrell, the Harmon Foundation was unable to ascertain their location. Reyneau's portrait of Mary Church Terrell was acquired by the National Portrait Gallery from the artist's descendants in 1996.

With the exception of the Charles Drew portrait, which was graciously loaned to the National Portrait Gallery for the exhibition "Breaking Racial Barriers," the portraits illustrated in the following section represent the entire collection of paintings donated by the Harmon Foundation in 1967. To provide a sense of historical context, the portraits that were displayed in the original 1944 exhibition at the Smithsonian Institution include excerpts from the original labels that accompanied them. As the majority of these unique testimonial labels were composed by socially and politically admired personalities, they were used by the foundation to further enhance the audience's admiration of the sitters.

Marian Anderson

A great artist, a great woman and a great citizen. Her incomparable talent, her beauty, and magnificent dignity have endeared her to the music loving world. When she sings it's not only the voice of her race one hears but the voice of America.
—Cornelia Otis Skinner

Arturo Toscanini claimed that contralto Marian Anderson had a voice that came along "once in a hundred years." When one of her music teachers first heard her sing, the richness of her talent moved him to tears. But because she was black, Anderson's prospects as a concert singer in this country were initially quite limited, and she experienced most of her early professional triumphs in Europe. Eventually, however, the magnitude of her talent won her broad recognition in the United States as well, and when she began touring regularly in this country in 1935, she was quickly acknowledged to be the world's greatest contralto. By the time Anderson retired in the mid-1960s, she was regarded as a national treasure.

Laura Wheeler Waring's extraordinary love of music, especially classical and opera, and her enduring admiration of Marian Anderson are both skillfully expressed in this formal portrait of the singer. Waring first saw Anderson on stage on April 16, 1916, during one of her extensive European concert tours. Waring was so moved by Anderson's performance that later that evening she wrote in her diary, "The 'Messiah' was very fine. Marian Anderson's contralto was beautiful. She won lots of praise." Waring's admiration of the talented singer remained strong a full twenty-seven years after first

hearing Anderson in concert. Mary Beattie Brady related to Alain Locke a conversation that she once had with Waring about her aspirations as an artist. "When I talked to Mrs. Waring she stated that one of her great problems has been to get important people in her own group to sit for her. . . . Her great desire is to do Marian Anderson." Waring's dream became reality when in 1944 she spent the summer painting the regal figure of Marian Anderson at her farm.

Anderson's pose reflects the calm and graceful stance of a seasoned singer patiently waiting for the applause to die down before bursting forth into song. Behind Anderson is a window framing a landscape with three crosses, symbolizing the death of Christ on Calvary.

MARIAN ANDERSON
1897–1993
Laura Wheeler Waring
Oil on canvas, 1944
National Portrait Gallery
Gift of the Harmon Foundation

Marian Anderson

Although Laura Wheeler Waring had painted the first portrait of Marian Anderson for the Harmon Foundation in 1944, Betsy Graves Reyneau had also aspired, for a number of years, to capture the image of the world-renowned singer in paint. Mary Beattie Brady recalled, *Mrs. Reyneau had hoped to do Marian Anderson herself, but she said she felt Mrs. Waring wanted to do her for this exhibit and it was highly important to make every effort so that she could. At a later date, if Miss Anderson were interested, she could do a portrait of her herself.* Eleven years later, this second portrait of Anderson was painted by Reyneau for the Harmon Foundation's collection. It documented her historic concert at the Lincoln Memorial, an event that was scheduled after the Daughters of the American Revolution had refused to let Anderson perform at its Constitution Hall because of her race. This incident caused an outpouring of public sympathy, which made Anderson a potent symbol in the struggle for racial tolerance.

Sixteen years after the concert, Reyneau probably relied upon photographs of it to reconstruct the setting. This second portrait, created after the exhibition formally ended, may have been commissioned by the foundation as an eventual replacement for the Waring portrait.

MARIAN ANDERSON
1897–1993
Betsy Graves Reyneau
Oil on canvas, 1955
National Portrait Gallery
Gift of the Harmon Foundation

Claude A. Barnett

Claude A. Barnett founded the Associated Negro Press (ANP), the largest and longest-lived news service covering subjects of interest to black citizens in the United States. Born in 1889 in Sanford, Florida, Barnett resided in Chicago for most of his life. Between 1904 and 1906, he attended Tuskegee Institute, where he acquired a long-lasting admiration for its founder, Booker T. Washington, and his principles of self-help and black capitalism. After graduation, Barnett returned to Chicago and in 1919 established the ANP. This placed him in the center of the black political arena, giving him wide influence and connections. His many activities included serving on the publicity committee of the Colored Voters Division of the Republican National Committee during Herbert Hoover's 1928 presidential campaign, serving for more than thirty years on Tuskegee's board of trustees, assisting the Democratic administration's Conference of Presidents of Negro Land Grant Colleges in drawing the attention to the needs of black colleges, and, with Frederick Douglass Patterson of Tuskegee Institute, advising the Department of Agriculture on the effectiveness of federal programs relating to black farmers.

Barnett also used his status as head of the ANP to promote desegregation in the armed forces and oppose racial segregation of blood donors. During the Harmon Foundation exhibition's tour, Barnett served as an adviser. His expertise in publicity and promotion proved invaluable to the project's success.

CLAUDE A. BARNETT
1889–1967
Betsy Graves Reyneau
Oil on canvas, circa 1953
National Portrait Gallery
Gift of the Harmon Foundation

Richmond Barthé

During the 1930s and 1940s, Richmond Barthé was the most widely exhibited and honored of the artists associated with the foundation. He actively exhibited his work with the foundation between 1929 and 1935. Throughout his career, Barthé maintained special interests in racial themes, portraiture, the theater, and religion.

Reyneau painted Barthé working on one of his religious paintings, *The Christ*. For more than a year, Barthé had worked intermittently on this figure. He hoped to portray a sculpted figure of a "universal" Christ—"one that will depict the ideals of Jews, Christians, Whites, Negroes, and all races and nationalities." Upon its completion, Barthé's work was erected in an African American church in Montgomery, Alabama. The church received the sculpture favorably and anticipated that it would wield tremendous social influence. *Pittsburgh Courier* columnist Ted Le Berthon wrote of the statue, "His significance, in this Stone summoning of His spirit, is that He will Make anyone feel inferior. Whites who think of themselves as racially superior to Negroes will, I suspect, see Him and come away unable to feel superior to anyone."

Mary Beattie Brady, an avid supporter of Barthé and his work, had planned to debut Reyneau's portrait of him in Chicago, where she had scheduled a Catholic group, under the Archbishop, to participate in the opening festivities. Reyneau did not complete the portrait in time, however, and it debuted at another venue.

RICHMOND BARTHÉ
1901–1989
Betsy Graves Reyneau
Oil on canvas, 1946
National Portrait Gallery
Gift of the Harmon Foundation

Mary McLeod Bethune

Born to slaves on a South Carolina farm, Mary McLeod Bethune struggled to acquire an education and then began her own work as a teacher alongside the pioneer black educator Lucy Laney. Subsequently, "on a dollar and sixty-five cents and a prayer," she founded and then directed Bethune-Cookman College in Daytona Beach, Florida. Describing her for the Harmon Collection exhibition, Channing Tobias summed her up as "not only the outstanding woman of her race, but, by general consent, one of the outstanding women of the world."

Reyneau's portrait of Bethune illustrates the strength, forthrightness, and convictions of a woman who firmly believed that education was the primary route to racial uplift. Bethune was sitting for Reyneau as well as for sculptor Ruth Brall at the time of this portrait's creation. In the background is a picture of the first building of the Daytona Literary and Industrial School for Training of Negro Girls, which later became Bethune-Cookman College. The four-story building was named Faith Hall, partly in honor of the chapel at Bethune's alma mater, Scotia Seminary, and partly because it exemplified what could be accomplished with faith. The cane in her hand was not for walking, but was a prop, as she believed it gave her "swank." Following a visit to Switzerland in 1927, where she had used an alpenstock for climbing and became fascinated with its many uses, she always had a cane or a walking stick. The globe in front represents Bethune's interest in the dissemination of knowledge and the integration of African Americans into American life.

MARY McLEOD BETHUNE
1875–1955
Betsy Graves Reyneau
Oil on canvas, 1943
National Portrait Gallery
Gift of the Harmon Foundation

Jane Matilda Bolin

Bolin, the first black woman in the United States to be appointed to a judgeship, was only thirty-one years old when Mayor Fiorello La Guardia chose her, in 1939, for a ten-year term on the Domestic Relations Court of the City of New York.

A Wellesley College graduate, Bolin was also the first black woman to receive a law degree from Yale University. She began her career as an attorney in her family's law firm in Poughkeepsie and, after her marriage in 1933 to Ralph E. Mizelle, practiced law with him under her maiden name. A Republican in politics, Bolin ran unsuccessfully for a seat in the New York State Assembly in 1936 and the following spring was appointed to the Corporation Counsel's office in New York City. Two years later, at the New York World's Fair, La Guardia swore her in as judge.

A dedicated activist for civil and children's rights and education, Bolin served on numerous boards, including those of Wiltwyck School for Boys, Dalton School, the Child Welfare League of America, New Lincoln School, United Neighborhood Houses, Neighborhood Children's Center, and the local and national NAACP. She also became a member of the Committee on Children of New York City, the Scholarship and Service Fund for Negro Students, the Urban League of Greater New York, and the Committee Against Discrimination in Housing. In January of 1944, Betsy Graves Reyneau traveled to New York to paint Bolin's portrait.

JANE MATILDA BOLIN
Born 1908
Betsy Graves Reyneau
Oil on canvas, 1944
National Portrait Gallery
Gift of the Harmon Foundation

Arna Bontemps

Author, librarian, and educator Arna Bontemps was truly a product of the Harlem Renaissance. Born in Alexander, Louisiana, Bontemps graduated from Pacific Union College in 1923 and then moved to New York City, where he soon became a recognized personality in the elite circle of African American artists and intellectuals of the Harlem Renaissance. Langston Hughes, Jean Toomer, James Weldon Johnson, and Countee Cullen were among those with whom Bontemps associated. In 1926 he was awarded the Alexander Pushkin Award for *Golgotha Is a Mountain* and received *Crisis* magazine's poetry prize the following year. Between 1923 and 1938, he taught in private schools, and in 1943 he became the librarian at Fisk University in Nashville.

Bontemps was greatly admired for his work as a compiler and anthologist of black literature. Included among his many publications are *An Anthology of Negro Poetry for Young People*, *The Book of Negro Folklore*, and *American Negro Poetry*.

ARNA BONTEMPS
1902–1973
Betsy Graves Reyneau
Oil on canvas, 1953
National Portrait Gallery
Gift of the Harmon Foundation

Ralph Johnson Bunche

Although Ralph Bunche's success in providing a permanent cease-fire and a peaceful settlement between the Arab and Jewish factions in the Near East in 1949, while simultaneously renewing the world's confidence in the United Nations as an influential and competent organization, were the major vehicles that launched him into the international spotlight and contributed to his receipt of the Nobel Peace Prize in 1950, these were not by any means his only accomplishments. In fact, the Ralph Bunche represented in this painting had as yet to accomplish these feats. In 1948, when Betsy Graves Reyneau completed this portrait, he was best known for his work for the State Department, where he was then associate chief of the Division of Dependent Area Affairs. Bunche had first been approached regarding a position in the State Department in 1944, after high-ranking officers filed enthusiastic reports on his intelligence work at the outbreak of World War II. Despite his reputation "as the foremost authority on colored peoples of the world," Bunche's appointment had received immediate opposition upon the discovery of his racial background. It was blocked for six months, until Secretary of State Cordell Hull discovered the true reason behind the delay and personally telephoned Bunche to offer him the job. This marked the first time in history that an African American had been given a desk-level position in the State Department.

Reyneau's portrait of Bunche suggests his work in the State Department through the inclusion of a map of Africa and Asia in the background. Reyneau has captured the essence of the cool, analytical, diplomatic Bunche, down to his characteristic cigarette.

RALPH JOHNSON BUNCHE
1904–1971
Betsy Graves Reyneau
Oil on canvas, 1948
National Portrait Gallery
Gift of the Harmon Foundation

Harry Thacker Burleigh

Burleigh's ascent to the position of baritone soloist at the St. George Episcopal Church in New York City was not entirely smooth. Dr. William S. Rainsford, then rector of the of the church, recalled that he "broke the news" to the St. George's choir *that I was going to have for a soloist a Negro, Harry Burleigh. Then division, consternation, confusion, and protest reigned for a time. I never knew how the troubled waters settled down. Indeed, I carefully avoided knowing who was for and who against my revolutionary arrangement. Nothing like it had even been known in the church's musical history. The thing was arranged and I gave no opportunity for its discussion.* In addition to the accolades Burleigh received for his musicianship in the St. George's choir, he also spearheaded the preservation of Negro spirituals at a time when many blacks wanted to forget them and the conditions from which they arose. Burleigh believed that music was "a powerful instrument for international understanding." In the *New York Herald Tribune* Burleigh was praised as one whose *life was one continuing flow of music; creative, imaginative, and almost always touched with the beauty and power of the Negro Spirituals. Music helped to design for* [him] *personally an existence that knew a full share of fulfillment. But the music that he made as a composer and singer was even more important in what it did for others.* Waring was a longtime friend of Burleigh.

HARRY THACKER BURLEIGH
1886–1949
Laura Wheeler Waring
Oil on canvas, circa 1946
National Portrait Gallery
Gift of the Harmon Foundation

William Ayers Campbell

Born at the Tuskegee Institute, Cadet William
Campbell trained there during World War II at
the special facilities established for black pilots
and technicians and graduated on July 3, 1942. Betsy
Graves Reyneau wrote about him, *Capt. Campbell of
the Ninety-ninth Pursuit Squadron was the first Negro pilot to
drop a bomb. He fought at Pantelleria, Sicily, Salerno, Anzio.
He flew as much as twelve hours a day during the critical days
when it seemed as if the troops at Salerno would be pushed back
into the sea. They were saved from complete disaster by the air
umbrella of the planes. He was sent home having completed his
missions, but asked to be sent back immediately as he wished to
fight as long as a white or Negro flier still faced the enemy. I
painted him at the Tuskegee Air Base, on his short furlough. He
is now at the European Front again.*

The portrait was painted in June 1944. Campbell's
father, Reyneau's escort, had suggested that she use
Campbell as a model for her symbolic portrait of
African American participation and heroism in the
war effort. As Campbell was only on leave for a day
or two, Reyneau organized a photography session
and choreographed several poses of Campbell in
full flight gear at a Tuskegee army airfield.

WILLIAM AYERS CAMPBELL
Born 1917
Betsy Graves Reyneau
Oil on canvas, 1944
National Portrait Gallery
Gift of the Harmon Foundation

Elmer Anderson Carter

Carter was born in Rochester, New York, where his father was a Methodist minister. He grew up in New York State, attended Harvard from 1908 to 1912, and subsequently taught at Prairie View State College in Texas. During World War I he served with the 92nd Division of the American Expeditionary Force in France.

After the war, Carter became executive secretary of the Urban League in Columbus, Ohio, before taking the same position in St. Paul and Minneapolis. Moving to New York City in 1928 to join the staff of the league's publication, *Opportunity, Journal of Negro Life,* he was its editor for fourteen years until 1942. Serving on the New York State Unemployment Insurance Appeal Board from 1937 to 1945, he was appointed a member of the New York State Commission Against Discrimination in 1945, and was the first African American to serve as its chairman.

ELMER ANDERSON CARTER
1890–1973
Betsy Graves Reyneau
Oil on canvas, before 1950
National Portrait Gallery
Gift of the Harmon Foundation

George Washington Carver

Scientist and Saint.

Whose clear vision perceived in simple plants materials he transformed into products useful for nourishment and beauty.

Always proclaiming kindly goodwill, generously giving the results of his patient research; saying his skill came from the constant inspiration of almighty God, who showed him the secrets of the loveliness of creation.

—William Jay Schieffelin

Born into slavery at the end of the Civil War, George Washington Carver exhibited an interest in plants as a child. By the late 1890s, after overcoming the dual obstacle of slender means and racial discrimination in seeking an education, he became the director of agricultural teaching and research at Alabama's Tuskegee Institute. There, his laboratory investigations led to the discovery of more than 450 new commercial products—ranging from margarine to library paste—that could be made from the peanut, the sweet potato, and various other cultivated plants. In the process, Carver demonstrated, for many southern farmers, the wisdom of diversifying in place of their soil-exhausting practice of relying mainly on cotton for their prosperity, and he himself became known as the "miracle worker."

Carver accepted a multitude of honors in the course of his career, but he consistently balked when artists sought to commemorate his accomplishments with a portrait. In 1942, however, he so admired Betsy Graves Reyneau's likeness of Edward Lee that he consented to pose for her. Reyneau's portrait of Carver is not only the last portrait painted of the great scientist before his death three months later, but is also the only known portrait painted of Carver from life. It reveals him in the midst of his favorite hobby, the cross-pollination of a hybrid amaryllis that he had developed.

GEORGE WASHINGTON CARVER
1864–1943
Betsy Graves Reyneau
Oil on canvas, 1942
Transfer from the National Museum of American Art
Gift of the George Washington Carver Memorial
Committee of the Smithsonian Institution, 1944

Betsy Graves

Aaron Douglas

A major artist of the Harlem Renaissance movement, Aaron Douglas was born in Topeka, Kansas. He worked in Detroit's automobile and glass factories to earn college tuition, and received a bachelor of fine arts degree from the University of Nebraska in 1922. Two years later Douglas moved to New York, "feeling himself drawn to Harlem by newspaper articles reporting the flowering of black cultural awareness." There he met and studied with the German artist Winold Reiss, who encouraged him to celebrate his racial heritage and introduce African motifs and themes into his paintings.

Considered by many historians as "the father of Black American Art," Douglas was a frequent contributor to *The Crisis* magazine and was the only African American artist featured in Alain Locke's classic anthology of black writers, *The New Negro* (1925). Douglas is best remembered for his illustrative collaboration with author James Weldon Johnson in his book of poetry, *God's Trombones: Seven Negro Sermons in Verse.*

Reyneau painted Douglas's portrait in front of *Song of the Towers,* the fourth in a series of four murals Douglas had painted in 1934 under the sponsorship of the Works Progress Administration. The series traces African Americans' history from their origins in Africa, through slavery, emancipation, and the great migration from the rural South to the industrialized, urban North. The *Song of the Towers* addresses African American entry into the northern cities. Positioned in front of his creation, Douglas strikes a dignified pose in his artist's smock, his pipe in hand.

AARON DOUGLAS
1899–1979
Betsy Graves Reyneau
Oil on canvas, 1953
National Portrait Gallery
Gift of the Harmon Foundation

Betsy Graves

Charles Richard Drew

*Surgeon and scientist. A brother of mankind and a lover of
freedom and truth. He labored industriously from 1938–1940
on the problems of blood preservation in the department of surgery
at the Presbyterian Hospital, New York. He was recalled from
Washington to act as medical supervisor of the Blood Plasma for
Britain. He was appointed the director of the first American Red
Cross Blood plasma Bank at the Presbyterian Hospital. The
success of this trial bank made possible the great undertaking
of the American Red Cross in furnishing plasma for the Armed
Forces of the United States.*

—John Scudder, M.D.

Charles Drew began his pioneering work with blood
plasma during his tenure as the first black surgical
resident at the Presbyterian Hospital in New York
City. Under the direction of Dr. John Scudder, the
hospital had organized a study of the human body's
fluid balance and blood chemistry, and the use of
blood transfusion to lessen postoperative shock.

In 1940, Drew received a cablegram from Dr. John
Beattie, then director of the research laboratories of
the Royal College of Surgeons in London, asking
him to secure five thousand ampules of dried plasma
for transfusion, to be used for the ever-increasing
numbers of wounded British citizens and soldiers.
Within a short time, Drew had organized the Blood
Transfusion Association to send plasma to Britain,
and the crisis in war-torn England's hospitals was
averted. A year later, Drew became medical director
of the American Red Cross's blood-donor project,
and it was largely thanks to his expertise that so
many lives were saved during World War II.

Drew left the Red Cross shortly after the organization ordered that all non-Caucasian blood be stored
separately, and he returned to teach at Howard
University and Freedmen's Hospital. In 1944, Drew
received the NAACP's Spingarn Medal for his work on
the British and American blood and plasma projects.

Charles Richard Drew, 1904–1950
Betsy Graves Reyneau, oil on canvas, 1953
National Portrait Gallery
Gift of the Harmon Foundation

The Harmon Foundation commissioned two
portraits of Drew from Reyneau during the
exhibition's tour. The first, created from life in 1944,
was purchased by Chicago physician Theodore
Lawless. It was donated to the National Red Cross
in 1959, in Drew's memory. The Harmon Foundation then commissioned a replacement portrait,
which Reyneau created posthumously from a
photograph taken by Washington photographer
Robert S. Scurlock in the late 1940s.

CHARLES RICHARD DREW
1904–1950
Betsy Graves Reyneau
Oil on canvas, 1944
The American National Red Cross
Gift of Sigma Pi Phi Fraternity

William Edward Burghardt Du Bois

Born in Great Barrington, Massachusetts, February 23, 1868. Distinguished American man of letters; a leading authority on the history of the Negro in this country and in Africa; most influential exponent in our generation of Negro rights. As Professor at Atlanta University for over twenty-five years and Editor of the Atlanta University Studies, Director of Publications of the National Association for the Advancement of Colored People, Editor of the Crisis *and of* Phylon, *founder of Pan-African Congresses, and in many other positions he has rendered outstanding service. His literary essays have brought him wider recognition even from those who have differed from some of his conclusions. His scholarly books in the fields of Negro history, biography, and sociology, from the appearance of the* Suppression of the Slave Trade—*his Harvard Ph.D. thesis in 1896—through* Black Folk: Then and Now *and* Dusk of Dawn *(1940) are a record of achievement that merits the profound gratitude of all thoughtful Americans. A man of independence, large intellectual ability, great moral courage, and public spirit, he has mellowed with the years, and now, after the battles of a lifetime in behalf of justice for his race, he deserves well of the Republic and the world.*

—Anson Phelps Stokes

W.E.B. Du Bois was a respected sociologist and historian, but he exerted his greatest influence as a strategist in the early civil rights movement. In 1905, rejecting those who claimed that full equality for African Americans must come gradually, Du Bois became a founder of the Niagara Movement, which called for an end to racial discrimination immediately. Four years later, he was helping to found the National Association for the Advancement of Colored People and for many years served as editor of its magazine, *The Crisis.*

Increasingly skeptical of his country's ability to crush racism, and accused of disloyalty during the McCarthy era as a result of his Communist sympathies, Du Bois was thoroughly alienated from America by the mid-1950s. In 1962 he expatriated himself to Ghana in the hope of reviving there "an ancient African Communism" based on black spiritual unity.

In 1953, the Harmon Foundation removed Du Bois's portrait from the traveling exhibition. Although the foundation maintained that this was to make room for newer portraits, many African Americans believed that it had been removed because of his alleged affiliation with the Communist party. Director of the Associated Negro Press Claude Barnett wrote to Mary Beattie Brady, *It is with great regret that I learn you have removed Dr. Du Bois' portrait from the group. Audiences everywhere would wish to see his portrait and it lessens the fabric of the whole not to have him in. The fact is, despite the charges which have been levelled against him because of his plain speaking, he commands the respect and appreciation of most people, certainly within our group.*

WILLIAM EDWARD BURGHARDT DU BOIS
1868–1963
Laura Wheeler Waring
Oil on canvas, not dated
Gift of Mr. Walter Waring in memory of his wife,
Laura Wheeler Waring, through the Harmon Foundation

Jessie Redmon Fauset

Jessie Fauset, the most published novelist of the Harlem Renaissance, was living in retirement in Montclair, New Jersey, when Laura Wheeler Waring painted her portrait for the Harmon collection. Her four books, *There is Confusion* (1924), *Plumb Bun* (1929), *The Chinaberry Tree* (1931), and *Comedy: American Style* (1933), exposed Americans to "a great group of Negroes of education and substance who are living lives of quiet interests and pursuits."

The daughter of an African Methodist Episcopal minister, Fauset grew up in Philadelphia and graduated from Cornell University in 1905. She received a master's degree in French from the University of Pennsylvania and went on to study at the Sorbonne. For fourteen years she taught French and Latin at what became Dunbar High School in the District of Columbia. From 1919 to 1926 Fauset was the indispensable associate of W.E.B. Du Bois in the publication of the NAACP magazine *The Crisis.* Persuading Du Bois that creative writing could be a source of racial uplift, Fauset cultivated the talents of young poets and novelists. Langston Hughes considered her to be one of three persons "who midwifed the so-called New Negro literature into being."

Laura Wheeler Waring and Fauset were old friends when she painted Fauset's portrait for the Harmon Foundation. Both native Philadelphians, Waring and Fauset were closely associated in Paris in 1914, and were good friends thereafter. It may have been this friendship that influenced the Harmon Foundation to include Fauset in its portrait collection, as her celebrity, which had reached its apex during the Harlem Renaissance, had significantly declined by the mid-1940s.

JESSIE REDMON FAUSET
1882–1961
Laura Wheeler Waring
Oil on canvas, 1945
National Portrait Gallery
Gift of the Harmon Foundation

Lester Blackwell Granger

Social scientist and executive director of the National Urban League, Granger was born in Newport News, Virginia. Educated at Dartmouth College, New York University, and the New School for Social Research, in 1930 he went to Los Angeles to organize the Urban League. In 1934 he joined the Urban League staff in New York as business manager for *Opportunity, Journal of Negro Life,* and as head of the Worker's Education Bureau. He became executive secretary of the league in 1941 and served as its head for twenty years.

An outspoken critic of discrimination against African Americans during the Second World War, Granger was honored by the Congress of Industrial Organizations (CIO) in 1943 for his work in race relations. Appointed after the war as special adviser to Secretary of the Navy James Forrestal, to review the Navy's programs of racial integration, he was awarded the Distinguished Civilian Service Award, the Navy's highest civilian decoration, in December 1945. In 1946, in a nationwide poll conducted by the trustees of the Schomburg Collection of Negro Literature and History in the New York Public Library, he was named one of eighteen Americans who had contributed toward better race relations. A prolific author of articles and pamphlets, Granger was awarded several honorary degrees, and after his retirement from the Urban League in 1961, he became a visiting professor at Dillard University in New Orleans.

LESTER BLACKWELL GRANGER
1896–1976
Betsy Graves Reyneau
Oil on canvas, 1950–1951
National Portrait Gallery
Gift of the Harmon Foundation

William Henry Hastie

William Henry Hastie gave up a Federal Judgeship to accept his present position of Dean of the Howard University Law School, where he felt that he could render a greater public service by training young men to fill the growing need for Negro Lawyers equipped not only to practice but to join the struggle for judicial protection of the civil rights and liberties of Negroes under the Constitution. In that struggle Dean Hastie and his Law School colleagues and former students have already played a notable part, participating in the conduct and argument of a number of important cases, including several before the U.S. Supreme Court, the last of which was the recent Texas primary case. Dean Hastie is a graduate of Amherst College, where he was Phi Beta Kappa, and of the Harvard Law School, where he was elected an editor of the Harvard Law Review—the most coveted honor in the School. He has served as Assistant Solicitor of the Interior Department and as Civilian Aid to the Secretary of War. He is still under forty, and his career of public service, already a distinguished one, is still in its creative stage. We shall hear more of the courageous and talented American in the years to come.

—L. K. Garrison

Hastie's portrait, sensitively rendered by Reyneau, exudes an aura of self-assuredness, dignity, and self-motivation especially sought after in sitters by the Harmon Foundation. Indeed he was, as stated by Assistant Secretary of the Interior Oscar L. Chapman, "a man of tolerance and good will, fully appreciative of the dignity of the human spirit, and devoted to the principles and ideals which are the keystone to democratic living."

WILLIAM HENRY HASTIE
1904–1976
Betsy Graves Reyneau
Oil on canvas, 1943–1944
National Portrait Gallery
Gift of the Harmon Foundation

Anna Arnold Hedgeman

Lecturer, consultant, author, activist, and sociologist, Anna Arnold Hedgeman spent her lifetime in hard work and dedication. Born on July 5, 1899, in Marshalltown, Iowa, and reared in Anoka, Minnesota, Hedgeman experienced racism at an early age when a three-year-old white girl inquired, "Anna, are you really a nigger?" The incident remained a painful memory throughout Hedgeman's life and may have helped motivate her long career in social activism. After graduating in 1922 from Hamline University in Minnesota, where she was its first African American student, she went on to Rust College, an African American college in Holly Springs, Mississippi. Overwhelmed by southern white hatred, she taught there for only one year. Returning north, where she secured a position in 1924 with the black branch of the YWCA in Springfield, Ohio, she encountered a different, yet just as disturbing, brand of racism. "I met the sugar-coated segregated pattern of social work and housing in the North . . . the first week of my employment . . . in the fall of 1924 was one of appalled discovery of Northern segregation."

In 1926 she became executive director of a branch of the YWCA in New Jersey, and in 1927, in Harlem, became the secretary of the West 137th Street Branch of the YWCA. In the fall of 1933 she was briefly executive director of the Catherine Street Branch of the YWCA in Philadelphia.

In 1934 Hedgeman was hired by New York City's Emergency Relief Bureau, where she worked with blacks, Jews, and Italians. She then became the director of the black branch of the Brooklyn YWCA, where she organized a citizens' coordinating committee to seek provisional appointments for African Americans. She succeeded in expanding employment opportunities for black clerks in Brooklyn department stores. Her organizational tactics, however, which included picketing to change racist systems, proved too radical for the YWCA, and she resigned.

Unfettered by institutional policies, Hedgeman continued to lobby for political change and in 1944, Asa Philip Randolph appointed her executive director of the National Council for the Permanent Fair Employment Practices Commission in Washington, D.C. Four years later she was hired as executive director of a national citizens' committee to raise funds for Harry S. Truman's presidential campaign. In 1949 she joined the Federal Security Agency. Between 1954 and 1958, Hedgeman served as an assistant in the cabinet of New York Mayor Robert F. Wagner, and then worked as an associate editor and columnist for the *New York Age.*

Hedgeman was instrumental in the planning stages of A. Philip Randolph's March on Washington, which later joined forces with Martin Luther King and took place in August 1963.

Betsy Graves

Charles Hamilton Houston

The high ideals of service to humanity and intense liberalism which have characterized the career of Charles Houston have merited the esteem and admiration of mankind. He is a man of tolerance and good will, fully appreciative of the dignity of the human spirit, and devoted to the principle and ideals which are the keystone to democratic living.

—Oscar Chapman

Referred to posthumously in 1958 by Thurgood Marshall as "the First Mr. Civil Rights," Houston was born in Washington, D.C., and attended both Dunbar High School and Amherst College from which he graduated in 1915. After teaching at Howard University for two years and serving in the infantry in World War I, he entered Harvard Law School. He was the first African American elected to the *Harvard Law Review.* He received his degree in 1922, and was awarded a doctorate of juridical science the following year. Admitted to the Bar in the District of Columbia in 1924, Houston practiced law with his father in the firm that William H. Hastie joined in 1939. Also on the faculty of the Howard University School of Law, Houston gave up his legal practice to serve as vice-dean and then dean of the school. During these years he participated in important legal cases regarding civil rights issues.

In 1935 Houston joined the NAACP as its first full-time special counsel. He presented or helped prepare many important cases, including *University of Maryland v. Murray* (1936), in which he argued before Maryland's highest court for admission of African Americans to the University of Maryland Law School, and *Missouri ex. rel. Gaines v. Canada* (1938), in which he argued before the Supreme Court to establish minority access to equal legal education. Returning to private practice in 1940, he continued to perform extensive work in the public interest. As general counsel of the Association of Colored Railway Trainmen and Locomotive Firemen and of the International Association of Railway Employees, he won major antidiscriminatory cases on their behalf. Serving on President Truman's Fair Employment Practices Committee, he resigned in 1945 over the discriminatory employment practices of the Capital Transit Company. A member of the American Council on Race Relations, in 1948 he helped prepare successfully argued Supreme Court cases that denied federal and state court protection for restrictive property covenants.

After his death at the age of fifty-four, he was awarded the NAACP's Spingarn Medal.

Charles Hamilton Houston
1895–1949
Betsy Graves Reyneau
Oil on canvas, 1943–1944
National Portrait Gallery
Gift of the Harmon Foundation

Charles Spurgeon Johnson

The first black president of Fisk University, from 1946 to 1956, Charles Johnson was a respected scholar, sociologist, educator, and administrator. The son of former slaves, young Johnson was largely self-taught when he entered Wayland Academy in 1909. With a strong background in the classics, he earned an A.B. degree from Virginia Union (1917) and a second bachelor's degree from the University of Chicago (1919), where he majored in social science.

From 1921 to 1928 Johnson headed the National Urban League's division of research and investigation. He founded and was first editor of *Opportunity* magazine, the official Urban League journal, which promoted African American talent in literature, art, sports, and other fields of endeavor. Under his guidance, *Opportunity* sponsored contests and distributed prizes for black writers and artists.

Johnson was among twenty educators sent to Japan in 1946 at the request of General Douglas MacArthur to advise on the reorganization of the educational system of that country. That same year he was also appointed as one of the ten United States delegates to the first session of the United Nations Educational, Scientific and Cultural Organization in Paris and to the second session in Mexico City.

In addition to his work in the field of education, Johnson was also a dedicated civil and social activist. From 1943 to 1948, he served as director of the Race Relations Division of the American Missionary Association and co-director of the Race Relations Program of the Julius Rosenwald Fund. Among his scholarly published works are *The Negro in Chicago* and *The Negro in American Civilization.*

CHARLES SPURGEON JOHNSON
1893–1956
Betsy Graves Reyneau
Oil on canvas, 1953
National Portrait Gallery
Gift of the Harmon Foundation

James Weldon Johnson

James Weldon Johnson, inspired poet and man of letters, successful song writer, distinguished diplomat and public servant, wise statesman, enlightened and courageous leader of his race and great American gentleman.

By his writings he made America aware of its shortcomings in its treatment of his race and of the priceless gifts that the Negro has made to our common civilization and by his life he illustrated that greatness cannot be limited by race or color.

—Arthur B. Spingarn

The author of "Lift Every Voice and Sing" (often called "the Negro National Anthem"), James Weldon Johnson had a long career as a creative writer, black leader, teacher, lawyer, diplomat, and executive secretary of the NAACP. Through his writing he protested racial injustice, encouraged black achievement, and added immeasurably to the wealth of American literary art.

A native of Jacksonville, Florida, Johnson attended Atlanta University through graduate school, receiving his M.A. in 1904. Returning home in the hope of establishing himself as a southern community leader, Johnson became principal of the grammar school, studied law, and in 1901 became the first African American admitted to the Florida Bar, but he did not remain in Florida for very long. Forming a creative partnership with his younger brother Rosamond, a writer of popular music, he began to write lyrics. They moved to New York and found fame as the ragtime songwriting team of Cole and Johnson Brothers.

While in New York, Johnson befriended Charles Anderson, a black Republican leader and confidant of Booker T. Washington. In 1906, through this connection, Johnson was appointed United States Consul to Venezuela and subsequently to the same post in Nicaragua. During these six years, he wrote and published *The Autobiography of an Ex-Colored Man* (1912). He then wrote the column "Views and Reviews" for the black weekly paper the *New York Age,* addressing such issues as residential segregation, lynching, and the necessity of racial pride.

In 1916, Joel Spingarn, chairman of the National Association for the Advancement of Colored People, asked Johnson to serve as a field secretary for the seven-year-old organization. In four years Johnson helped increase the NAACP membership from 9,000 to approximately 90,000. Johnson in turn was appointed head of the NAACP in 1920, and for the next ten years he led the organization in its fight for racial equality. In 1930 he retired and spent the eight remaining years of his life writing and teaching.

Waring's unique background in her posthumous portrait of Johnson recalls the imagery in "Creation," the best-known and most often recited of the poems in his most famous literary work, *God's Trombones: Seven Negro Sermons in Verse* (1927).

JAMES WELDON JOHNSON
1871–1938
Laura Wheeler Waring
Oil on canvas, 1943
National Portrait Gallery
Gift of the Harmon Foundation

Mordecai Wyatt Johnson

Leading Educator of Race. Keen of thought, pure of mind, profound in wisdom. Far-seeing Champion of Human Justice. Great Orator whose spoken words charm the mind, quicken the intellect, and establish wisdom to those who listen and learn.

—Walter Gray Crump

On September 1, 1926, Mordecai W. Johnson became the thirteenth president of Howard University and the first black to hold that post. From a modest background, Johnson earned bachelor of arts degrees from Morehouse College and the University of Chicago, and a master of sacred theology degree from Harvard University. Rabbi Stephen S. Wise named him "one of the ten greatest religious leaders in the country."

The undisputed head of Howard University for thirty years, Johnson used his gifts of oratory, wit, and diplomacy to guide the university through years of development. He won for it its reputation as the "Capstone of Negro Education." In 1929 the NAACP awarded him the distinguished Spingarn Medal "for persuading the Federal Congress to legalize," with the passage of H.R. 8466, "the annual appropriation for Howard University." Under Johnson's administration, a twenty-year plan for educational and physical development was adopted and sources of private philanthropy were tapped; new dormitories and new laboratories were built; the teaching staff was doubled; salaries were boosted; faculty tenure was advanced; scholarly publication was encouraged; and academic standards were raised.

Betsy Graves Reyneau, who spent several months at Howard in 1943 painting likenesses of a number of the nation's leading black scholars, portrayed Johnson two years past the halfway mark of his thirty-year tenure.

MORDECAI WYATT JOHNSON
1890–1976
Betsy Graves Reyneau
Oil on canvas, 1943
National Portrait Gallery
Gift of the Harmon Foundation

John Andrew Kenny

John Andrew Kenney was a leader in the medical profession, especially in providing training and medical services to the African American community. He was born in Albemarle County, Virginia, and graduated from Hampton Institute in 1897. He received his medical degree from Leonard Medical College at Shaw University in Raleigh, North Carolina, in 1901, and served an internship at Freedman's Hospital in Washington, D.C. From 1902 to 1925 he was resident physician at Tuskegee Institute, where he was also medical director and chief surgeon at the John A. Andrew Memorial Hospital and Nurses Training School. While at Tuskegee, he became active in the National Medical Association, serving as its secretary (1904–1912), president (1912–1913), and a founder and early business manager of its *Journal*. He became editor of the *Journal* in 1916 and held that position for more than thirty years. At Tuskegee he also was personal physician to Booker T. Washington and George Washington Carver.

After he received approval from President Warren Harding in 1923 to hire African American staff members for the new Veterans Administration hospital, he was forced to leave Tuskegee because of threats of violence from the Ku Klux Klan. He then went into private practice in Newark, New Jersey, where he founded the Kenny Memorial Hospital, which he deeded in 1934 to the Booker T. Washington Community Hospital Association. He returned to Tuskegee in 1939 to serve as medical director of the John A. Andrew Memorial Hospital until 1944.

JOHN ANDREW KENNY
1874–1950
Betsy Graves Reyneau
Oil on canvas, 1943–1944
National Portrait Gallery
Gift of the Harmon Foundation

Theodore K. Lawless

A gifted physician, Theodore K. Lawless was one of the first to use radium as a treatment for cancer. Born in Louisiana and educated in Alabama, Lawless received his medical degree in Chicago in 1919. After serving in the Medical Corps Reserve in World War I, he studied abroad, and after that was a Rosenwald Fellow at Columbia University, Massachusetts General Hospital, and Harvard Medical School.

Lawless opened a medical practice in Chicago in 1924, and taught at Northwestern Medical School. He was a member of the Cook County Prison Welfare Commission and the Chicago Board of Health, and of various college boards of trustees. In 1929, Dr. Lawless received the Harmon Award for outstanding work in medicine, and in 1954, he was awarded the NAACP's Spingarn Medal.

In addition to his medical work, Lawless also served as president of the Service Federal Savings and Loan Association in Chicago, which was active in financing black business enterprises, and of the 4213 South Michigan Corporation, which promoted low-cost housing.

Lawless's support of the Harmon Foundation's portrait collection was extended beyond his services as a sitter, when in 1958 he purchased Reyneau's portrait of Dr. Charles Drew. He donated the portrait to the National Red Cross in memory of Drew's lifetime achievements in the fields of science and medicine.

THEODORE K. LAWLESS
1892–1971
Betsy Graves Reyneau
Oil on canvas, 1953
National Portrait Gallery
Gift of the Harmon Foundation

Alain Leroy Locke

He has mastered western thought and can teach the most subtle doctrines of the philosophers. As a critic of the arts and of life, he has earned the gratitude of all lovers of clarity and beauty. But he is greatest in the magnanimous patience with which he waits for the rest of mankind to discover what his race has done and can do in the future.

—Lyman Bryson

An interpreter of black cultural achievements, Alain Locke is recognized as the authority on his race's contributions to the humanities. A Harvard Phi Beta Kappa graduate and the first black Rhodes Scholar at Oxford University, he also studied in Germany before returning to Harvard to earn his Ph.D. in 1918.

Although a native Philadelphian, Locke had his greatest impact upon African American culture during his tenure at Howard University in Washington, D.C. At Howard, Locke conveyed to his students the value of the fine arts. He started a drama group, the Howard Players, and a literary magazine, the *Stylus.* Locke's influence gained national attention in 1925 when he edited the now-classic *The New Negro,* an anthology of African American writings that aimed "to document the New Negro culturally and socially—to register the transformations of the inner and outer life of the Negro in America that have so significantly taken place in the last few years."

Throughout his life, Locke grappled with the issue of how African Americans could achieve full social integration without sacrificing their own cultural legacy. At the time of his death, he was preparing a major work, *The Negro in American Culture.*

Locke served as both a subject and an adviser for the Harmon Foundation portrait collection. Brady and Reyneau would often solicit his opinion for possible sitters, as well as strategies through which to promote the exhibition. Although Reyneau met with Locke on several occasions, he apparently did not sit for his portrait. Painted from a photograph, Locke's portrait represents him as a quiet, dignified scholar. According to Mary Beattie Brady, Director of the Harmon Foundation, he was purposefully depicted in his "Oxford jacket" to particularly emphasize that achievement.

ALAIN LEROY LOCKE
1885–1954
Betsy Graves Reyneau
Oil on canvas, 1943–1944
National Portrait Gallery
Gift of the Harmon Foundation

Betsy Graves

Joe Louis

Boxer Joe Louis had one of his greatest moments on June 22, 1938, when he faced the German Max Schmeling in a match to regain the world heavyweight championship. Louis knocked Schmeling out in a little over two minutes and, in the process, won the admiration of many Americans, who saw his triumph as the ultimate debunking of Hitler and his Nazi theories. Sports historian Edwin B. Henderson describes Louis's public image: *A halo was spun over him. He was good to his mother. He bought a home for her in Detroit. He paid back to the city of Detroit $270 drawn by his family in relief during the Depression. He did not smoke. He did not drink. That was the Joe Louis the public came to know.*

Reyneau painted this portrait of Joe Louis while he was still at the pinnacle of his fame. He is posed as though fighting (a position frequently utilized during this time for boxing publicity photographs) in a position that emphasizes both his grace and his furious power. Louis's talents as a boxer, his strong moral convictions, and his love for his country launched him into the spotlight as the first black heavyweight to win the support of the entire boxing-loving public. He once stated about his career, "I think it is part of my job as a champion to try to help America and my own people."

JOE LOUIS
1914–1981
Betsy Graves Reyneau
Oil on canvas, 1946
National Portrait Gallery
Gift of the Harmon Foundation

Betsy Graves

Thurgood Marshall

In the African American struggle to end racial discrimination in the United States, no one played a more salient role than Thurgood Marshall. Born in Baltimore, Marshall attended public schools, and in 1925 he entered the historically black Lincoln University near Chester, Pennsylvania. After graduation, he returned to Maryland to enroll in the University of Maryland's Law School, but his application was denied because of his race. He then promptly enrolled in the law program at Howard University.

Marshall attended Howard's Law School during Charles Houston's tenure as its dean. Inspired by Houston's vision of developing the university into a "West Point of black leadership," Marshall graduated in 1933 with highest honors and established a law practice in Baltimore. In 1935 he was invited to join the legal staff of the NAACP under its chief counsel, Charles Houston, Howard's former dean. Ironically, Marshall's first significant victory, *Pearson v. Murray,* awarded African Americans the right to study at the University of Maryland Law School.

In 1938 Marshall succeeded Charles Houston as national special counsel responsible for all cases involving citizenship rights for Negroes. In 1950, Marshall was named director-counsel of the NAACP's Legal Defense and Educational Fund, where he spearheaded the elimination of practices and laws that prevented blacks from enjoying their full rights of citizenship. Among his greatest triumphs was the United States Supreme Court case *Brown v. Board of Education,* in which, in 1954, he and his associates successfully challenged the legality of racial segregation in the nation's public schools.

Appointed to the United States Court of Appeals in 1962, Marshall later served as the nation's first African American solicitor general. In 1967 he became the first African American to sit on the Supreme Court, where he distinguished himself as a spokesman for racial equality and the rights of the underprivileged. Always modest when it came to talking about his achievements, Marshall observed, at his retirement in 1991, that he wanted to be remembered simply as a man who had done "what he could with what he had."

THURGOOD MARSHALL
1908–1993
Betsy Graves Reyneau
Oil on canvas, 1956
National Portrait Gallery
Gift of the Harmon Foundation

Mary Lee Mills

Lieutenant Commander Mary Mills dedicated
twenty-six years of her career to the United States
Public Health Service, establishing maternal and
child health clinics, nursing schools, and public
health programs around the world.

Mills received early training as a nurse at Lincoln
Hospital in her native state of North Carolina. She
continued her education in New York, where she
obtained certification from the Lobenstine School
of Midwifery and both bachelor's and master's
degrees in nursing from New York University. From
1946 until 1966, she served as a public health nurse
for the United States Public Health Service in
Liberia, Lebanon, Cambodia, Vietnam, and Chad.
Her exceptional skill and dedication to public
health issues brought her many awards and
honorary degrees, including the American Nurses
Association's 1972 award for her contributions to
integration in the nursing profession. Mills also
received the Harmon Foundation Award in 1952,
an honorary doctor of science degree from
Tuskegee Institute in 1956, and the Rockefeller
Public Service Award for human resources development in 1971. She was the first woman to receive
the Rockefeller award, the highest privately
sustained honor for a career civil servant.

Reyneau's portrait of Mills was first unveiled in
January 1953, during the meeting of the American
Nurses Association in New York. At that time, Mills
was considered one of the finest ambassadors for
America's nurses. As Harmon Foundation director
Mary Beattie Brady noted, the American Nurses
Association, as one of the first national professional
associations to incorporate an African American–
based organization into their total association
membership, had taken "the lead in wiping out
color lines."

MARY LEE MILLS
Born 1912
Betsy Graves Reyneau
Oil on canvas, 1952
National Portrait Gallery
Gift of the Harmon Foundation

Hugh Nathaniel Mulzac

In 1942, against overwhelming odds, Captain Hugh Mulzac became the first African American naval officer to command an integrated crew during World War II. Born on St. Vincent Island, British West Indies, Mulzac entered the Swansea Nautical College in South Wales to prepare for a seaman's career while in his twenties. He became an American citizen in 1918, and continued his training at the Shipping Board in New York. He earned his captain's rating in the Merchant Marines in 1920, but racial prejudice denied him the right to command a ship. He sailed instead as a mate, working his way up through the ranks to chief cook.

Later Mulzac was offered the command of a ship with an all-black crew. He refused, declaring that "under no circumstances will I command a Jim Crow vessel." Twenty-two years passed before Mulzac would again receive an offer to command a naval ship. During World War II, his demand for an integrated crew was finally met, and he was put in command of the S.S. *Booker T. Washington*. With its crew of 18 nationalities, the *Booker T. Washington* made 22 round-trip voyages in five years, and carried 18,000 troops to Europe and the Pacific. On the day his ship was launched, Mulzac recalled, *Everything I ever was, stood for, fought for, dreamed of, came into focus that day. . . . The concrete evidence of the achievement gives one's strivings legitimacy, proves that the ambitions were valid, the struggle worthwhile. Being prevented for those twenty-four years from doing the work for which I was trained had robbed life of its most essential meaning. Now at last I could use my training and capabilities fully. It was like being born anew.*

The *Booker T. Washington* was turned back over to the Maritime Commission by the Luckenbach Steamship Company in 1947. After his ship was retired, Mulzac was unable to get a similar assignment. During his forty years in the shipping industry, Mulzac had been a seaman, quartermaster, bos'n, third mate, second mate, and chief officer.

HUGH NATHANIEL MULZAC
1886–1971
Betsy Graves Reyneau
Oil on canvas, 1946
National Portrait Gallery
Gift of the Harmon Foundation

Peter Marshall Murray

Dr. Peter Murray utilized his immense talents as a surgeon, hospital administrator, and author to fight against racial discrimination in the medical profession.

Murray spent his early childhood in Houma, Louisiana, on his grandparents' farm, while his parents worked in New Orleans. In 1900, at the age of twelve, Murray joined his parents. After receiving his education at New Orleans University (later Dillard), he moved to Washington, D.C., where he worked in the civil service while attending the College of Medicine at Howard University. Completing his degree in 1914, he was appointed by Howard's College of Medicine as an instructor in surgery and later promoted to assistant surgeon-in-chief of Freedman's Hospital. Murray also established a private practice and became a medical inspector for the District of Columbia public schools. In 1921, Murray moved to New York City and in 1928 began working at Harlem Hospital Clinic. He became its director of gynecological service, and in 1953 he served as president of the Medical Board and director of obstetrics and gynecology at the Sydenham Hospital.

Murray both overcame and fought to eradicate many racial barriers throughout his career. He helped desegregate Harlem Hospital during the 1930s and Sydenham Hospital in the 1950s. As the first African American delegate in the American Medical Association, he worked diligently to eliminate racism in all of its component societies, including those in the Deep South.

Reyneau's portrait of Murray highlights his contribution to the fight for racial integration in the medical profession.

PETER MARSHALL MURRAY
1888–1969
Betsy Graves Reyneau
Oil on canvas, 1956
National Portrait Gallery
Gift of the Harmon Foundation

Frederick Douglass Patterson

Frederick D. Patterson was the founder of the
United Negro College Fund, and served as president of the Tuskegee Institute in Alabama from
1935 to 1953. A native of Washington, D.C.,
Patterson was educated in veterinary science, and
was first hired to be the head of the veterinary
division at Tuskegee in 1928. He also served as head
of the School of Agriculture before becoming
president of the Institute.

A constant concern for Patterson and the leaders of
other black colleges was fund-raising. In 1943,
Patterson proposed the creation of a consortium of
colleges that would raise money for their shared
benefit. In 1944, the United Negro College Fund was
founded, with twenty-seven member colleges.
By 1947, Patterson was a member of President
Truman's Commission on Higher Education, which
advocated direct federal aid to colleges and universities as well as the elimination of segregation. At
his death, Frederick Patterson was lauded as one
who "broke new ground for minority students and
was always looking ahead into the next decade for
new ways to finance education."

FREDERICK DOUGLASS PATTERSON
1901–1988
Betsy Graves Reyneau
Oil on canvas, 1955
National Portrait Gallery
Gift of the Harmon Foundation

Asa Philip Randolph

Many civil rights activists dismissed Asa Philip Randolph in his later years as too conservative in his approach to breaking down the barriers of racial segregation. But as a black labor organizer and pioneer of the twentieth-century civil rights movement, his militancy once led his opponents to regard him as the "most dangerous Negro in America." Though negative, that characterization reflected the tremendous impact Randolph had in reshaping this country's racial relationships.

Born in 1889 in Crescent City, Florida, the son of an African Methodist minister, Randolph grew up in an environment that valued hard work and education. He attended high school at the historic Cookman Institute in Jacksonville. At the age of twenty-two, he migrated north to New York City, where he worked at odd jobs during the day and attended college at night, studying political science, economics, and philosophy. In 1917, he and his friend Chandler Owen founded the militant and revolutionary magazine *The Messenger*. Dedicated to the principles of labor unionism and socialism among blacks, *The Messenger* was soon noticed by white politicians, such as J. Edgar Hoover, who in 1919 described it in a Senate Judiciary Committee report as "the most able and most dangerous of all the Negro publications."

By the mid-1920s, however, Randolph realized that African Americans were not going to be easily converted to socialism, and he began to channel his energies into trade-union organizing. In 1925 he accepted the position as general organizer of the newly formed Brotherhood of Sleeping Car Porters. As editor of *The Messenger*, Randolph used it to disseminate the propaganda of this organization,

and it soon became the Brotherhood's official publication. Randolph and his publication became catalysts for the integration of American labor, and played a decisive role in pressing for the establishment in 1941 of the Fair Employment Practices Committee, the first federal effort to eliminate racial discrimination from the workplace.

In the 1940s, Randolph spearheaded the campaign to force a presidential order to integrate the country's armed forces. A March on Washington, which he organized in 1941 to protest the exclusion of blacks from the armed forces, was prevented by Roosevelt, who issued Executive Order 8802 abolishing segregation in defense industries. Randolph continued to press for the elimination of Jim Crow laws in all sectors of the military. On June 22, 1948, he announced the formation of a League for Non-Violent Civil Disobedience Against Military Segregation, which would conduct a campaign of noncompliance if an antidiscrimination order was not issued by August 16. President Harry Truman issued Executive Order 9981 on July 26, 1948, which ended legal discrimination within the armed services.

ASA PHILIP RANDOLPH
1889–1979
Betsy Graves Reyneau
Oil on canvas, 1945
National Portrait Gallery
Gift of the Harmon Foundation

Paul Robeson

Friend of Mankind, lover of freedom, defender of the oppressed.

A great American who has grown to be a world leader. His voice is heard with delight, his words are fraught with good will, his art is acclaimed as glorious. He inspires a zeal to do justly and to banish prejudice. Let us learn of him that all men are brothers.
—William Jay Schieffelin

A singer, actor, athlete, orator, and linguist, Paul Robeson was a man blessed with immense talent and intelligence. Educated at Rutgers and Columbia Law School, he began practicing law in 1923. But his theatrical talents were so impressive that while he was still at Columbia, he was offered the lead role in the professional production of *Taboo*. After playing the lead in Eugene O'Neill's *The Emperor Jones* in 1924, his short career as a lawyer ended.

Betsy Graves Reyneau's portrait of Paul Robeson portrays him in one of his greatest roles, that of Shakespeare's Othello. But his resentment of racial discrimination eventually led him into affiliations that many equated with Communism. As a result, during the militantly anti-Communist crusade that overtook this country following World War II, he was bitterly denounced, and his career came largely to an end. When this happened, even this portrait became an object of indignation. When the picture arrived in Boston in 1950, the mayor ordered it barred from the show.

That same year, after Robeson's passport was revoked by the State Department, the Harmon Foundation succumbed to public pressure and permanently removed the Robeson portrait from the exhibition. Director Mary Beattie Brady said, *I hope the time will come when it will be practical to again emphasize Mr. Robeson's achievements as a singer and an actor, and if later events prove him to be a true patriot of this country . . . the portrait will be available . . . . My decision is based on the fundamental purpose of the exhibit which was to reflect American leadership of the highest type in terms of Americans of Negro Ancestry.*

Unfortunately, the exhibition was dismantled in 1954, four years before the State Department, under worldwide pressure and protest and following a Supreme Court ruling, returned his passport.

PAUL ROBESON
1898–1976
Betsy Graves Reyneau
Oil on canvas, 1944
National Portrait Gallery
Gift of the Harmon Foundation

Edith Spurlock Sampson

Time and time again, Edith Sampson overcame the barriers of racial segregation to become the first black woman appointed as a judge in Illinois, the first woman to graduate from the Loyola University Law School in Chicago, the first black delegate to the United Nations, and the first black person to hold an appointment with the North Atlantic Treaty Organization.

Sampson grew up in Pittsburgh, Pennsylvania, as part of a large family. Although her education was periodically interrupted because she had to leave school and work to earn her tuition, she studied at the Columbia University School of Social Work, the John Marshall Law School, and Loyola University. In 1927, she was awarded the LL.M., becoming the first woman in that university's history to have received the degree. That same year, she passed the Bar and in 1934 was admitted to practice before the Supreme Court.

Sampson practiced both law and social work throughout her life. In 1949, she was selected to represent the National Council of Negro Women in the "America's Town Meeting of the Air" radio program. Traveling through twelve countries with twenty-five other national, civic, cultural, welfare, and labor leaders to debate political issues of world concern, Sampson found the appointment to be a life-altering experience. She declared, "After visiting and talking with the peoples of other countries, I knew that I could never make my law practice the primary business of my life; I would have to devote myself to the cause of world brotherhood and peace."

In 1950, appointed by President Truman to serve as an alternate United States delegate to the fifth regular session of the General Assembly of the United Nations, Sampson became a strong advocate for the world's underprivileged children. In 1961 and 1962 she was appointed by the Vice President to serve on the United States Citizens Commission on the North Atlantic Treaty Organization and in 1964 and 1965 was a member of the Advisory Committee on Private Enterprise in Foreign Aid.

In 1962, Sampson was elected associate judge of the Municipal Court of Chicago. She was the first black woman in the United States to gain the position through such an election.

EDITH SPURLOCK SAMPSON
1901–1979
Betsy Graves Reyneau
Oil on canvas, 1953
National Portrait Gallery
Gift of the Harmon Foundation

Ruth Janetta Temple

Ruth Temple was the first black woman physician to practice in Los Angeles and was a lifelong advocate for public health issues. At her death, the Los Angeles County public health clinic was renamed in her honor for her efforts to fund public health clinics in that city during the 1940s.

Temple grew up in Los Angeles, and received her medical degree from the College of Medical Evangelists in 1918. Her efforts to improve community health services dated from the beginning of her career. After five years with the Los Angeles City Maternity Service, she began to specialize in obstetrics and gynecology. In 1941, the city gave her funding to pursue a master's degree in public health from Yale University. Upon her return, she was appointed the first health officer of Los Angeles. From 1946 until 1962, Temple was the director of special programs for the city Health Department, and received many awards for her work.

She was active until her death at age ninety-one, urging the prevention of illness through diet and lifestyle changes. In 1949, a Harmon Foundation press release noted that Temple had been singled out by *Look* magazine as "one of them most forward-looking public health officers of any U.S. city."

RUTH JANETTA TEMPLE
1892–1984
Betsy Graves Reyneau
Oil on canvas, 1948
National Portrait Gallery
Gift of the Harmon Foundation

Howard Thurman

Howard Thurman was a prominent clergyman and advocate for religious institutions that served the poor and disadvantaged. Although he was ordained as a Baptist minister in 1925, Thurman chose to teach at Morehouse College and Spelman College in Atlanta until 1932, when Mordecai Johnson asked him to teach at Howard University in Washington, D.C. While on sabbatical from Howard in 1935, Thurman journeyed through India, Burma, and Ceylon, and was inspired to create a church that would transcend racial, sectarian, and economic boundaries. He continued to teach at Howard, and served as dean of the chapel there until 1944, when his dream was realized as he became co-pastor, with Reverend Alfred Fisk, of the Church for the Fellowship of All Peoples in San Francisco. For nine years Thurman shared the pastorate at this church, founded, as he noted, to make Christianity "live for the weak as well as the strong—for all peoples whatever their color, whatever their caste."

In 1945 Thurman published *Deep River: An Interpretation of Negro Spirituals.* By 1953, he had been named dean of the chapel and professor of religion at Boston University School of Theology, where he was the first full-time African American faculty member.

Howard Thurman
1900–1981
Betsy Graves Reyneau
Oil on canvas, 1945
National Portrait Gallery
Gift of the Harmon Foundation

Channing Heggie Tobias

He is one of the elder statesmen of the colored group in this country, honored by all for his fair, constructive, and Christian approach to the complicated problems of race, and for embodying in his own life courtesy and thoughtfulness in all public and private relations. There are few men whose judgment and cooperation are more sought after on Boards of Trustees to which are entrusted great gifts in the interest of education, religion, and philanthropy.

—Anson Phelps Stokes

Channing Tobias was an outspoken advocate for interracial cooperation. After a few years as a professor of biblical literature at Paine College, where he had received his B.A., and having been ordained as a Methodist minister, Tobias joined the YMCA, which was a springboard for his many activities on behalf of the struggle for racial equality. His considerable gifts as a speaker and writer gained him a national and international career with that organization, as senior secretary of the Colored Men's Department (1923–1946). He was a member of the board of trustees of Howard University (1931–1953), Paine College, and Hampton Institute, and was—along with Ralph Bunche, Claude Barnett, and Frederick D. Patterson—an esteemed board member of the NAACP from 1943 to 1953, when he became chairman of that board, a position he held until 1959. He was an alternate delegate to the Sixth General Assembly of the United Nations in 1951, where he spoke in favor of "freedom from segregation in all forms."

Tobias received the Harmon Award in 1928, the Spingarn Medal for Distinguished Achievement in 1948, and an honorary LL.D. from New York University in 1950, the first conferred upon an African American by that institution.

CHANNING HEGGIE TOBIAS
1882–1961
Betsy Graves Reyneau
Oil on canvas, 1943–1944
National Portrait Gallery
Gift of the Harmon Foundation

Walter Francis White

Walter White was born in Atlanta, Georgia, where he remained to undertake his preliminary and college studies at Atlanta University. Upon his graduation in 1916, he enrolled in graduate school at the College of the City of New York. From 1918 to 1931, he served in the position of assistant executive secretary of the National Association for the Advancement of Colored People (NAACP). Upon the retirement of James Weldon Johnson, White took over the leadership of the organization, serving as the NAACP's executive secretary, a position he held until his death.

As a boy, White had witnessed the Atlanta Race Riot in 1906. The horrors of the mob violence later motivated him to risk his life investigating for the NAACP 41 lynchings, 8 race riots, and numerous Ku Klux Klan cross-burnings. Throughout his career, White diligently fought for civil rights legislation, lectured on the evils of lynching, and battled to end discrimination and segregation in travel and education.

In addition to his crusading work with the NAACP, White also authored numerous books and publications that related "race prejudice, segregation and Jim Crowism." A John Simon Guggenheim Fellow for European study and writing, White won the Harmon Award in Literature (1929) for *Rope and Faggot*, and received the Spingarn Medal in 1937. Critics found his writing "impartial, fair, scholarly, yet impassioned enough to stir the American public to realize not only what lynching does to the Negro body but to the soul of whites."

WALTER FRANCIS WHITE
1893–1955
Betsy Graves Reyneau
Oil on canvas, 1945
National Portrait Gallery
Gift of the Harmon Foundation

Helen Adele Johnson Whiting

Mrs. Whiting as one of the State Supervisors of rural education in Georgia, has been outstanding as an educator. She has written many books on negro folklore for children.

She has gained a national reputation for her faithful and progressive work. She had many opportunities to teach in the north, but she chose the field that she felt was most in need of good modern teaching, as did Dr. Carver.

—Betsy Graves Reyneau

Helen Adele Whiting worked in public education for more than twenty years to bring parity to African American elementary school curriculums, particularly in the South. She was noted for her efforts to make black children aware of their racial and cultural heritage.

Born in Washington, D.C., Whiting graduated from Howard University's Teachers College. After a few years of teaching experience, she was invited to head the Division of Drawing and Writing at Tuskegee Institute in 1912. Appointed a State Institute instructor the following year, Whiting traveled within the state of Alabama to lecture on primary teaching methods. After supervising practice teaching at Tuskegee Institute, Whiting attended Columbia University, where she received a master's degree in 1931. After supervising schools for blacks in Charlotte, North Carolina, and then for the state of Georgia, she became an instructor in education programs for Atlanta University.

Harmon Foundation director Mary Beattie Brady admired Whiting's work with southern teachers, particularly concerning the incorporation of African American history into school curriculums. In 1931, Brady wrote to Whiting, "I think these [programs] are of greatest importance in educational work among Negroes. Any outstanding work that is being done along these lines should certainly be brought to wider public attention." Whiting's achievements undoubtedly inspired the Harmon Foundation's commission of Reyneau to paint her portrait.

HELEN ADELE JOHNSON WHITING
1885–1950
Betsy Graves Reyneau
Oil on canvas, circa 1944
National Portrait Gallery
Gift of the Harmon Foundation

Paul Revere Williams

From his student days at the Polytechnic High School in Los Angeles, Paul Revere Williams aspired to be an architect, but was told "Who ever heard of a Negro architect?" Williams afterward related that he found his race to be "an incentive to personal accomplishment, an inspiring challenge. Without having the wish to 'show them,' I developed a fierce desire to 'show myself.'"

Williams worked his way through the University of California by teaching art until he became a certified architect in 1915. He continued his studies at the Los Angeles School of Art and Design and the Beaux Arts Institute of Design in New York. Following graduation, Williams searched through the Los Angeles telephone book until he found an architectural firm willing to take on a black drafts-man. Williams worked for large architectural firms until he gained sufficient experience in all branches of his profession to open his own office.

Williams's firm took on projects both large and small, working in a variety of architectural styles. Much of his firm's work was residential. Williams not only designed mansions for film stars such as Lon Chaney, Lucille Ball, and Tyrone Power, but also planned thousands of small houses in developments throughout California and Nevada. He wrote about his interest in attractive and comfortable housing for lower-income groups in two publications, *Small Homes for Tomorrow* and *New Homes for Today*.

Williams served on the Los Angeles City Planning Commission and the city's Municipal Housing Commission. Many of Williams's best-known works were commercial or public. He assisted in the design for the Los Angeles International Airport and the Los Angeles County Courthouse, and was the architect for a number of department stores, hotels, and churches in California and Nevada.

At the time Betsy Graves Reyneau painted his portrait, Williams had been a practicing architect for twenty-five years.

PAUL REVERE WILLIAMS
1894–1980
Betsy Graves Reyneau
Oil on canvas, 1948
National Portrait Gallery
Gift of the Harmon Foundation

Monroe Nathan Work

Director of Records and Research
Editor of the Negro Year Book
Tuskegee Institute

Probably the foremost American compiler of reliable information concerning the condition and progress of Negro Americans.

His "Bibliography of the Negro" is the authoritative volume on the subject.

Faithful, thorough, able, persistent and devoted, his services deserve the gratitude of the American people.
— Thomas Jesse Jones

In 1918 sociologist Monroe Nathan Work, whose chief labor was the compilation of "exact knowledge" of blacks in America and Africa, was nominated to receive the William E. Harmon Award for distinguished achievement among Negroes in education. "Because of his quiet and unassuming manner and his avoidance of anything that savors of pomp or show," wrote a Work supporter, "he might be overlooked were it not for his friends who appreciate the worth of the man and who desire to see his merit recognized." The award, a gold medal and an honorarium of $400, was presented to Work in recognition of "scholarly research and educational publicity through his periodic compilation and publication of the *Negro Year Book,* and his exhaustive *Bibliography of the Negro in Africa and America.*" In the latter, Work declared, "Every phase of Negro life and history is covered."

The North Carolina–born Work, the son of former slaves, was brought up on a farm in Illinois and studied sociology at the University of Chicago, where he received a master's degree in 1903. In 1908 Booker T. Washington offered him a position at Tuskegee Institute in Alabama, and it was there that Betsy Graves Reyneau found him in active retirement, engaged in expanding his bibliography, when she came to paint George Washington Carver in 1942.

MONROE NATHAN WORK
1866–1945
Betsy Graves Reyneau
Oil on canvas, 1942
National Portrait Gallery
Gift of the Harmon Foundation

Original Exhibition Venues, 1944–1954

1. MAY 2–28, 1944, National Collection of Fine Arts, Smithsonian Institution, Washington, D.C.
   Sponsored by George Washington Carver Memorial Committee, National Museum, Smithsonian Institution

2. OCTOBER 10–22, 1944, Detroit Institute of Art, Detroit, Michigan
   Sponsored by Detroit Interracial Committee, Committee on Popular Education

3. 1945, Grand Rapids Art Gallery, Grand Rapids, Michigan
   Sponsored by Grand Rapids Art Gallery

4. 1945, Battle Creek, Michigan
   Sponsored by Alpha Kappa Alpha Sorority, Altrusa Club of Battle Creek, American Association of University Women, American Legion Auxiliary, Battle Creek Business and Civic League, Battle Creek District, Michigan State Nurses Association, Battle Creek Gas Co., Battle Creek Women's Club, Carver Club, Christian Home Councils of the Seventh-Day Adventist Church, Circulus Club, Council of Church Women, Dardanelle Art Club, D.A.R., G.A.R., William H. Mason Fortress, General Foods Corp. Post Foods Division, Mrs. Lyle Griffen, Kiy-Klub, Lakeview Bank of Battle Creek, Ministerial Association, Mount Zion AME Church, NAACP, Negro College Women, Professional Business & Industrial Club of the Y.W.C.A., Parent Teachers' Association, Lincoln School, Washington, St. Philip Church, Second Baptist Church, Senior Women's Volunteers, Sportsman's Club, Study Culture Club, Theatre Guild, Ultra Art Club, Veterans of Foreign Wars Auxiliary, Alice V. Murphy, Post 565, Willing Aid, Woman's Christian Temperance Union, Women's League, Kellogg's

5. NOVEMBER 1945, Brooklyn Museum, Brooklyn, New York
   Sponsored by Brooklyn Museum

6. NOVEMBER 28, 1944–DECEMBER 1945, Roosevelt House of Hunter College, New York City
   Sponsored by the Toussaint L'Ouverture Club of Hunter College

7. JANUARY 4–29, 1946, Milwaukee Art Institute, Milwaukee, Wisconsin
   Sponsored by Milwaukee Art Institute and the Mayor's Committee

8. FEBRUARY 3–25, 1946, Chicago Historical Society, Chicago, Illinois
   Sponsored by group of six black sororities—Alpha Kappa Alpha, Delta Sigma Theta, Iota Phi Lambda, Phi Delta Kappa, Sigma Gamma Rho, Zeta Phi Beta, cooperating with the Chicago Historical Society

9. MARCH 6–APRIL 10, 1946, Cleveland Historical Society, Cleveland, Ohio
   Sponsored by Cleveland Museum of Art

10. 1946, Philadelphia, Pennsylvania
    Sponsored by Philadelphia Fellowship Commission

11. FEBRUARY 9–18, 1947, The Peale Museum, Baltimore, Maryland
    Sponsored by Association of Teachers in the Colored Schools of Baltimore and Peale Museum

12. MARCH 3–APRIL 15, 1947, Fort Wayne Art Museum, Fort Wayne, Indiana

You are invited to

An Exhibit of Portraits

OF DISTINGUISHED CITIZENS OF NEGRO HERITAGE

By

LAURA WHEELER WARING
and **BETSY GRAVES REYNEAU**

CHICAGO HISTORICAL SOCIETY
(North Avenue and Clark Street)

FEBRUARY 3rd THROUGH FEBRUARY 25th, 1946

Portraits of Dr. George Washington Carver, James Weldon Johnson, George Edmund Haynes, Jessie Redman Fauset, William Edward Burghart Du Bois, Dr. Mordecai W. Johnson, Mary McLeod Bethune, Marian Anderson, Harry T. Burleigh, William Henry Hastie, Dr. Charles Drew, Paul Robeson, Eugene Kinkle Jones, Helen A. Whiting, Asa Philip Randolph, Dr. John Andrew Kenney, Dr. Monroe Nathan Work, Chaning H. Tobias, Charles Hamilton Houston, Jane M. Bolin, Anna Arnold Hedgeman, Dr. Alaine Locke, Walter White

Sponsored by 1400 Chicago women, members of six Negro sororities, Alpha Kappa Alpha, Delta Sigma Theta, Iota Phi Lambda, Phi Delta Kappa, Sigma Gamma Rho, Zeta Phi Beta.

Co-Chairmen: Miss Louise C. Gaines
             Mrs. Helen B. Graham

Advisor: Claude A. Barnett

Endorsed by Edwin R. Embree, of the Mayor's Committee of Human Relations.

(No charge for the exhibit for children or adults, but on Sundays The Chicago Historical Society charges 30 cents admission for adults. Hours Sundays, 12:30 to 5:30; week days, 9:30 to 4:30.)

Sponsored by Fort Wayne Interracial Committee, Fort Wayne Art School and Museum, National Council of Catholic Women, Allen County Social Worker's Club, Pilot's Club, Federated Clubs of Wheatly Center, Delta Sigma Phi, Fort Wayne Art League, Y.W.C.A. Weekday Church School Teachers, Associated Churches, Inc., Fort Wayne Teachers' Association, Business and Professional Women's Club

13. APRIL 17–27, 1947, Toledo Museum of Art, Toledo, Ohio
    Sponsored by Toledo Museum of Art and Race Relations Committee of the Y.W.C.A.

14. MAY 7–JUNE 1, 1947, Carver Neighborhood Center, Kansas City, Missouri
    Sponsored by the Urban League, Carver Neighborhood Council, Council of Social Agencies, Greater Kansas City Industrial Union Council C.I.O., Kansas City Council of Colored Parents and Teachers, The Negro Chamber of Commerce, United Workers Club, Y.W.C.A., Y.M.C.A., Pan-Hellenic Council of Greater Kansas City

15. AUGUST 31–SEPTEMBER 30, 1947, Minneapolis Institute of Arts, Minneapolis, Minnesota
    Sponsored by Minneapolis Institute of Arts

16. OCTOBER 5–26, 1947, St. Paul Art Gallery and School of Art, St. Paul, Minnesota
    Sponsored by St. Paul Art Gallery and School of Art, St. Paul Council of Human Relations, Urban League

17. JANUARY 1948, Portland Art Museum, Portland, Oregon
    Sponsored by the Portland Museum and the NAACP

18. FEBRUARY 1948, California Palace of the Legion of Honor, San Francisco, California

19. MARCH 9–28, 1948, Fresno Memorial Auditorium, Fresno, California
    Sponsored by A.A.U.W. Art Section, "B" Street Community Center, El Clubo Del Mañana, Frances Harper Club, Fresno Republican Printery Co., Hollenbeck Bush Planing Mill Co., Incandescent Supply Co., Intercultural Fellow-

ship, Mt. Pleasant Baptist Church, NAACP, Progressive Social Club, Second Baptist Church, Valley Lumber Co., West Fresno Baptist Church, Weston Rouze Gallery, Wil-Lo-Se Club, Y.W.C.A. and the Fresno Art Council

20. APRIL 4–MAY 15, 1948, Art Gallery, Los Angeles, California
    Sponsored by Los Angeles Branch of the NAACP, Alpha Kappa Alpha Society, Allied Art League, a number of individuals, including the City Councilman, Christ Cosmopolitan Church, the East Side Community Center, the East Side Settlement Club, Pedro Fontilla, the Inter-denominational Ministers Alliance, Los Angeles Public Library, and a large number of individuals from lay and professional ranks

21. MAY 23–JUNE 19, 1948, Fine Arts Gallery in Balboa Park, San Diego, California
    Sponsored by San Diego Board of Education, Fine Arts Gallery of San Diego, and the NAACP

22. JUNE 20–JULY 24, 1948, Asilomar Hotel and Conference Grounds, Pacific Grove, California
    Sponsored by the Asilomar Hotel and Conference Grounds, and the Y.W.C.A.

23. 1948, Public Library, Pasadena, California
    Sponsored by Board of Education, NAACP, Art Institute, Junior League, and the library

24. 1948, Oakland Art Gallery, Oakland, California
    Sponsored by the A.F. of L. and the Oakland Art Gallery

25. SEPTEMBER 1948, Main Public Library, Long Beach, California
    Sponsored by the NAACP of Long Beach

26. OCTOBER 5–24, 1948, Santa Barbara Museum of Art, Santa Barbara, California
    Sponsored by Santa Barbara Museum of Art and a committee of local groups, probably including the Council for Civic Unity

27. NOVEMBER 1948, Recreation Park Clubhouse, Long Beach, California

PORTRAITS
of
OUTSTANDING AMERICANS
of
NEGRO ORIGIN

Dr. George Washington Carver
by
Betsy Graves Reyneau

FORT WAYNE ART MUSEUM

1026 W. Berry Street

MARCH 3   APRIL 15

28. DECEMBER 1949, San Luis Obispo Recreation Building, San Luis Obispo, California
   Sponsored by Council for Civic Unity

29. FEBRUARY 6–26, 1949, Jordan Junior High School, Palo Alto, California
   Sponsored by local church and civic groups, Y.M.C.A., Society of Friends, Palo Alto Fair Play Committee, Rotary Club, Kiwanis Club, Council for Civic Unity, Art Club and NAACP, Ministerial Association, Federated Negro Women, Stanford Art Gallery

30. OCTOBER 2–28, 1949, State Capitol, Salt Lake City, Utah
   Sponsored by Y.W.C.A., Y.M.C.A., NAACP, Salt Lake City Schools, A.A.U.W., Council for Civic Unity, B'nai Israel, Emerson Club of the Unitarian Church, State Department of Public Instructions, Salt Lake Council of Women, Salt Lake Ministerial Association, Men and Women of B'nai B'rith, Civic Center, Civic Study Club, Negro Women's Club, State Institute of Fine Arts, American Association for Childhood Education, Delta Kappa Gamma (teachers), Utah Labor's Joint Legislative Committee, and the Council for Civic Unity

31. FEBRUARY 5–25, 1950, Congregation B'nai Israel, Pontiac, Michigan
   Sponsored by Y.W.C.A., Y.M.C.A., Ministerial Association, Southwest Community Center, Boys' Club, Council of Pontiac Church Women, Council of Human Relations, Pillars Club, Women's Society of Christian Service of First Methodist Church, Fellowship of First Congregational Church, Family Service Center, Club of Pontiac Public Schools, General Richardson Chapter D.A.R.

32. MARCH 8–29, 1950, Dayton Art Institute, Dayton, Ohio

33. OCTOBER 1–30, 1950, Senate Chamber of the State Capitol, Hartford, Connecticut
   Sponsored by State of Connecticut (former Governor Chester E. Bowles) and cooperating groups

34. NOVEMBER 14, 1950, Boston Y.W.C.A., Boston, Massachusetts
   Sponsored by City of Boston and Y.W.C.A.

35. 1950, Tuskegee Institute, Tuskegee, Alabama
   Sponsored by NAACP and Tuskegee Institute

36. MAY 1953, City-County Building, Pittsburgh, Pennsylvania
   Sponsored by Mayor's Council for Civic Unity

37. Seattle Art Museum, Seattle, Washington

38. San Jose, California

EXHIBIT of OUTSTANDING NEGRO AMERICANS

May 7–June 1, 1947
2:00 to 9:00 P.M. Daily

•

Presenting

A collection of thirty-two oil portraits of distinguished Americans of Negro origin painted by Betsy Graves Reyneau and Laura Wheeler Waring.

Prepared by the Harmon Foundation, New York City.

•

Arranged by

CARVER NEIGHBORHOOD CENTER
and
URBAN LEAGUE OF KANSAS CITY
at
Carver Neighborhood Center, 1608 Campbell
Kansas City 8, Missouri

Notes on Sources

The following is a list of sources used in the Harmon Foundation portrait collection's biographical essays. Any additional information not found in these sources is located in the National Portrait Gallery's registrar's files.

MARIAN ANDERSON

Hine, Darlene Clark, ed., *Black Women in America: An Historical Encyclopedia.* Vol. 1. Brooklyn: Carlson Publishing Inc., 1993.

Flynn, James J. *Negroes of Achievement in Modern America.* New York: Dodd, Mead & Company, 1970.

Locke, Alain. Papers. Moorland-Spingarn Collection, Howard University, Washington, D.C.

Patterson, Lindsay, ed. *The Negro in Music and Art.* International Library of Negro Life and History. New York: Publishers Company, Inc., 1969.

Smith, Jessie Carney, ed. *Epic Lives: One Hundred Black Women Who Made a Difference.* Detroit: Visible Ink Press, 1993.

————. *Notable Black American Women.* Detroit: Gale Research Inc., 1992.

Waring, Laura Wheeler. Diary. Collection of Madeline Wheeler Murphy. Baltimore, Maryland.

Waring, Walter E. Interview by Madeline Wheeler Murphy. Philadelphia, Pennsylvania, May 25, 1973.

CLAUDE A. BARNETT

Barnett, Claude A. Papers. *The Associated Negro Press, 1918–1967.* Edited by August Meier and Elliot Rudwick. Part 1. Manuscript Division, Library of Congress, Washington, D.C.

Folkes, Karl C. *Negroes in Public Affairs and Government.* Edited by Walter Christmas. Vol. 2. Yonkers: Educational Heritage, Inc., 1966.

RICHMOND BARTHE

Locke, Alain. Papers.

Porter, James A. *Modern Negro Art.* Washington, D.C.: Howard University Press, 1992.

Reynolds, Gary A., and Beryl J. Wright. *Against the Odds: African-American Artists and the Harmon Foundation.* New Jersey: The Newark Museum, 1989.

MARY MCLEOD BETHUNE

Bowie, Walter Russell. *Women of Light.* New York: Harper & Row, 1963.

Daniel, Sadie Iola. *Women Builders.* Washington, D.C.: Associated Publishers, 1970.

Flynn. *Negroes of Achievement in Modern America.*

Hine, ed. *Black Women in America: An Historical Encyclopedia.* Vol. 1.

Ross, B. Joyce. *Black Leaders of the Twentieth Century.* Edited by John Hope Franklin and August Meier. Urbana: University of Illinois Press, 1982.

Smith, ed. *Notable Black American Women.*

JANE M. BOLIN

Hine, ed. *Black Women in America: An Historical Encyclopedia.* Vol. 1.

Locke, Alain. Papers.

Robinson, Wilhelmena S. *Historical Negro Biographies.* International Library of Negro Life and History. New York: Publishers Company, Inc., 1969.

Smith, ed. *Notable Black American Women.*

ARNA BONTEMPS

Hedgepeth, Chester M., Jr. *Twentieth-Century African American Writers and Artists.* Chicago: American Library Association, 1991.

RALPH JOHNSON BUNCHE

Flynn. *Negroes of Achievement in Modern America.*

Lindenmeyer, Otto J. *Negroes in Public Affairs and Government.* Negro Heritage Library. Edited by Walter Christmas. Vol. 2. Yonkers: Educational Heritage, Inc., 1966.

Robinson. *Historical Negro Biographies.*

Thomas, Henry, and Dana Lee Thomas. *50 Great Modern Lives.* New York: Hanover House, 1956.

HARRY THACKER BURLEIGH

Patterson, ed. *The Negro in Music and Art.*

ELMER ANDERSON CARTER

Fleming, James G., and Christian E. Burckel, eds. *Who's Who in Colored America.* 7th ed. Yonkers-on-Hudson: Christian E. Burckel & Associates, 1950.

Spradling, Mary Mace, ed. *In Black and White.* 3rd ed. Vol. 1. Detroit: Gale Research Inc., 1980.

Who Was Who in America, with World Notables, 1982–1985. Vol 8. Chicago: Marquis Who's Who, Inc.

GEORGE WASHINGTON CARVER

Locke, Alain. Papers.

Thomas and Thomas. *50 Great Modern Lives.*

Yost, Edna. *Modern Americans in Science and Technology.* New York: Dodd, Mead & Company, 1961.

AARON DOUGLAS

Huggins, Nathan Irvin. *Harlem Renaissance.* New York: Oxford University Press, 1971.

CHARLES DREW

Stratton, Madeline Robinson. *Negroes Who Helped Build America.* Boston: Ginn and Company, 1965.

Sterne, Emma. *Blood Brothers: Four Men of Science.* New York: Alfred A. Knopf, 1959.

W.E.B. DU BOIS

McDonnell, Robert W. *The Papers of W.E.B. Du Bois.* New York: Microfilming Corporation of America, 1981.

Metcalf, George R. *Black Profiles.* New York: McGraw-Hill Company, 1968.

Rodgers, Joel Augustus. *World's Great Men of Color.* Vol. 2. New York: Macmillan Publishing Co., Inc., 1972.

Rudwick, Elliot. *Black Leaders of the Twentieth Century.* Edited by John Hope Franklin and August Meier. Urbana: University of Illinois Press, 1982.

Wesley, Charles H. *The Quest for Equality: From Civil War to Civil Rights.* International Library of Negro Life and History. New York: Publishers Company, Inc., 1968

JESSIE R. FAUSET

Dannett, Sylvia G. L. *Profiles of Negro Womanhood.* Negro Heritage Library. Vol. 2. Yonkers: Educational Heritage, Inc., 1966.

Hine, ed. *Black Women in America: An Historical Encyclopedia.* Vol. 1.

Smith, ed. *Notable Black American Women.*

Wesley. *The Quest for Equality: From Civil War to Civil Rights.*

LESTER GRANGER

Rothe, Anna, ed. *Current Biography, 1946.* New York: H. W. Wilson Company, 1946.

New York Times Biographical Service. Vol. 7, no. 1. Obituary, January 9, 1976.

Spradling, ed. *In Black and White.* Vol. 1.

Who Was Who in America. Vol 6.

WILLIAM HENRY HASTIE

Lindenmeyer, Otto J. *Negroes in Public Affairs and Government.* Vol. 2.

Robinson. *Historical Negro Biographies.*

ANNA ARNOLD HEDGEMAN

Estick, Sheila M. *Negroes in Public Affairs and Government.* Negro Heritage Library. Vol. 1. Yonkers: Education Heritage, Inc., 1966.

Hine, ed. *Black Women in America: An Historical Encyclopedia.* Vol. 1.

Smith, ed. *Notable Black American Women.*

CHARLES HAMILTON HOUSTON

Garraty, John A., and Edward T. James, eds. *Dictionary of American Biography: Supplement Four, 1946–1950.* New York: Charles Scribner's Sons, 1964.

Logan, Rayford W., and Michael R. Winston. *Dictionary of American Negro Biography.* New York: W. W. Norton & Company, 1982.

Rothe, ed. *Current Biography: Who's News and Why, 1948.*

———. *Current Biography: Who's News and Why, 1950.* New York: H. W. Wilson Company.

Spradling, ed. *In Black and White.* Vol. 1.

Who Was Who in America. Vol. 3.

JAMES WELDON JOHNSON

Levy, Eugene. *Black Leaders of the Twentieth Century.* Edited by John Hope Franklin and August Meier. Urbana: University of Illinois Press, 1982.

Lindenmeyer. *Negroes in Public Affairs and Government.* Vol. 2.

Mordecai W. Johnson

Harmon Foundation Collection, Manuscript Collection, Library of Congress.

John Andrew Kenny

Kaufman, Martin, Stuart Galishoff, and Todd L. Savitt, eds. *Dictionary of American Medical Biography*. Vol. 1. Westport: Greenwood Press, 1984.

Theodore K. Lawless

Morais, Herbert M. *The History of the Negro in Medicine*. International Library of Negro Life and History. New York: Publishers Company, Inc., 1969.

Joe Louis

Henderson, Edwin B., and the editors of *Sport* magazine. *The Black Athlete: Emergence and Arrival*. International Library of Negro Life and History. New York: Publishers Company, Inc., 1969.

Robinson. *Historical Negro Biographies*.

Thurgood Marshall

Flynn. *Negroes of Achievement in Modern America*.

Lindenmeyer. *Negroes in Public Affairs and Government*. Vol. 2.

Metcalf. *Black Profiles*.

Robinson. *Historical Negro Biographies*.

Wesley. *The Quest for Equality: From Civil War to Civil Rights*.

Hugh Mulzac

Wesley. *The Quest for Equality: From Civil War to Civil Rights*.

Peter Murray

Logan and Winston. *Dictionary of American Negro Biography*.

Frederick Douglass Patterson

Who Was Who in America. Vol 6.

Asa Philip Randolph

Flynn. *Negroes of Achievement in Modern America*.

Quarles, Benjamin. *Black Leaders of the Twentieth Century*. Edited by John Hope Franklin and August Meier. Urbana: University of Illinois Press, 1982.

Robinson. *Historical Negro Biographies*.

Paul Robeson

Hughes, Langston, and Milton Meltzer. *Black Magic: A Pictoral History of the Negro in American Entertainment*. New Jersey: Prentice-Hall, Inc., 1967.

Rodgers, *World's Great Men of Color*. Vol. 2.

Edith S. Sampson

Folkes. *Negroes in Public Affairs and Government*. Vol. 1.

Hine, ed. *Black Women in America: An Historical Encyclopedia*. Vol. 2.

Smith, ed. *Notable Black American Women*.

Ruth Temple

Hine, ed. *Black Women in America: An Historical Encyclopedia*. Vol. 2.

Howard Thurman

Who Was Who in America. Vol. 6.

Channing Tobias

Feder, Irwin. *Negroes in Public Affairs and Government*. Negro Heritage Library. Ed. Walter Christmas. Vol. 1.

Robinson. *Historical Negro Biographies*.

Walter White

Robinson. *Historical Negro Biographies*.

Helen Adele Whiting

Harmon Foundation Collection, Manuscript Division, Library of Congress.

Paul Williams

Robinson. *Historical Negro Biographies*.

Paul Work

Harmon Foundation Collection, Manuscript Division, Library of Congress.

Wesley. *The Quest for Equality: From Civil War to Civil Rights*.

For Further Reading

Bearden, Romare, and Harry Henderson. *A History of African-American Artists from 1792 to the Present.* New York: Pantheon Books, 1993.

Berkeley Art Center. *Ethnic Notions: Black Images in the White Mind.* Berkeley: Berkeley Art Center Association, 1982.

Franklin, John Hope, and Alfred A. Moss Jr. *From Slavery to Freedom: A History of Negro Americans.* 6th ed. New York: Alfred A. Knopf, 1988.

Harley, Sharon. *The Timetables of African-American History.* New York: Simon & Schuster, 1995.

Johnson, Abby Arthur, and Ronald Maberry Johnson. *Propaganda and Aesthetics: The Literary Politics of Afro-American Magazines in the Twentieth Century.* Amherst: The University of Massachusetts Press, 1979.

Lewis, David Levering. *When Harlem Was in Vogue.* Oxford: Oxford University Press, 1989.

————. *W.E.B. Du Bois: Biography of a Race, 1868–1919.* New York: Henry Holt and Company, 1993.

Lueders, Edward. *Carl Van Vechten and the Twenties.* Albuquerque: University of New Mexico Press, 1955.

McElroy, Guy. *Facing History: The Black Image in American Art, 1710–1940.* Washington, D.C.: Corcoran Gallery of Art, 1990.

Martin, Francis John, Jr. "The Image of Black People in American Illustration from 1825–1925." (Ph.D. diss., University of California, 1986).

Parry, Ellwood. *The Image of the Indian and the Black Man in American Art.* New York: George Braziller, 1974.

Reynolds, Gary A., and Beryl J. Wright. *Against the Odds: African American Artists and the Harmon Foundation.* New Jersey: The Newark Museum, 1989.

Wintz, Cary D. *Black Culture and the Harlem Renaissance.* Houston, Texas: Rice University Press, 1988.

Acknowledgments

In 1967, the Harmon Foundation officially closed its doors for the final time, leaving behind a unique forty-five-year legacy of interracial cooperation and promotion of twentieth-century African American achievement. Upon its dissolution, the Harmon Foundation donated its collection to the National Portrait Gallery, with the intention that the forty-one portraits of distinguished American citizens would be publicly available on a permanent basis. Although well acquainted with the Harmon Foundation's work in the field of African American art through such publications as Gary A. Reynolds and Beryl J. Wright's *Against the Odds: African-American Artists and the Harmon Foundation* (1989), James A. Porter's *Modern Negro Art* (1943), and Romare Bearden and Harry Henderson's *A History of African American Artists from 1792 to the Present* (1993), I did not encounter any significant information regarding the Harmon Foundation's collection of African American portraits until I entered the National Portrait Gallery as a curatorial intern in the summer of 1995. I became so intrigued with the history of this pioneering and controversial exhibition that I decided to base my master's thesis on the subject. The catalogue *Breaking Racial Barriers: African Americans in the Harmon Foundation Collection* is in large part a result of my graduate research, which I could not have completed without the assistance, guidance, and generosity of a multitude of individuals.

Foremost on my list of acknowledgments is the late Dorothy Porter Wesley. Upon my arrival to the Washington, D.C., area, she welcomed me into her home and promptly instructed me on the importance of preserving and recording African American history and culture. For the wisdom, advice, and inspiration she imparted to me during the time we spent together, I dedicate this effort in her memory. I would also like to thank her daughter, Connie Uselac, who supported my early endeavors as a scholar by guiding me in my research through Mrs. Porter Wesley's collection of primary resource materials.

I am under special obligation to my mentor, David C. Driskell, and his family; he not only allowed me access to his archives, which proved an invaluable resource, but also counseled and supported me through the most difficult periods in my graduate studies. Additionally, I am deeply indebted to community activist and author Madeline Wheeler Murphy, the niece of artist Laura Wheeler Waring. Murphy's generosity with her collection of documents and with her own knowledge regarding her aunt was also a source of vital and much-appreciated information.

Among those who donated their time, knowledge, ideas, and scholarly encouragement to this project are my parents, Drs. John and Barbara Fleming, whose achievements in the fields of higher education and African American history are a daily inspiration; my thesis adviser and assistant professor of arts in the Diaspora at the University of Maryland, College Park, Dr. Juanita Holland, whose insightful suggestions have proved indispensable to my work; my thesis committee members, American art assistant professor Dr. Sally Promey and twentieth-century art assistant professor Dr. Jane Sharp, both from the University of Maryland; nineteenth-century European art professor June Hargrove, for encouraging me to reapply for a second internship at the National Portrait Gallery; Martin Luther King Jr. University Professor at Rutgers, David Levering Lewis, for his encouragement and assistance in helping me locate the manuscript repositories for many of the exhibition's sitters; and National Museum of American History Director Spencer Crew, for his words of inspiration and scholarly advice.

I also wish to thank the staff and administrators at the National Portrait Gallery who patiently guided me through my two internships as well as the very new, exciting, and rewarding experience of curating and writing this exhibition and catalogue. Although this project was the culmination of the efforts of many individuals throughout the gallery, I am especially appreciative of the biographical contributions, advice, and assistance from Ellen Miles, curator; Brandon Fortune, assistant curator, Margaret Christman, historian, and Dorothy Moss, administrative secretary, of the Department of Painting and Sculpture. Finally, appreciation is owed to Alan Fern, director, for his inspirational words of encouragement, Carolyn Carr, deputy director, and Beverly Cox, curator of exhibitions, for their assistance and support; Frances K. Stevenson, publications officer, and Dru Dowdy, managing editor, for their efficient and expert handling of the catalogue; and Suzanne Jenkins, registrar, for her able assistance in verifying the provenance of the W.E.B. Du Bois portrait.

Tuliza K. Fleming